Victim No More!

Robin Y. Cotè

DRAGONFIRE
PRODUCTIONS

Victim No More!
Robin Y. Cotè
Second Edition
Non-Fiction
ISBN: 978-0-9962020-2-2

This book is dedicated to those who have been affected by abusive situations and traumatic events. To all those who did not survive, we honor you in the best way we can...by sharing our stories and helping others in the process.

To my son Jeffrey, you are the reason I was able to get up each time I was knocked down. I would have given up if you weren't there, dependent upon me. You breathed life into me in more ways than I could have ever imagined, and I am eternally grateful!

A huge thank you to all those who have supported me along the way. Your kind words and encouragement kept me going, even during the toughest of times. It's not easy reliving these moments.

A heartfelt thank you to Troy Barnes for telling me the one thing which helped me to accomplish putting this book out. Your words will forever stay with me my friend!

A special thank you to Brian Jackson and Debra Shiveley Welch for getting me back in the game and on the right path!

To my tribe, you know who you are. I love you dearly, and I'm so lucky to have you in my life. Thank you for being there and believing in me!

And to my angel Sara, thank you for watching over me. I hope I make you proud and I promise I will keep up the good fight, honoring your memory.

FOREWORD

I first met Robin in late 2011. I was on a holiday from Australia and we were introduced through mutual friends. This was my first trip to the USA, and my initial impression of her was very clear. I had found, what I considered to be, a true American woman. She was blonde and sassy, confidant, hard-working, and had presence in a room.

You knew Robin was there. She didn't hide in the corner.

We were friends from that moment on.

The following evening, I was introduced to Jeff, Robin's son, and it was clear that family was a major driver in her life. There was so much love in this family. The bond between them was a beautiful thing to admire.

I never knew of Robin's past until 2014, when she told me that she was putting together a book of her life, entered one piece at a time via blog entries. I started to follow these posts and was genuinely shocked that this wonderful person, someone I hold great respect for, had endured a life of personal hell. This strong woman with the infectious personality hadn't always been that way. Her life had been a never-ending physical and mental struggle.

When Robin asked me if I would write the foreword for her life story, I decided to stop reading the constant entries and wait until the book was complete. I wanted to devour the book as a whole, and I'll be honest, there were times when the content was tough reading. I write horror-themed novels, but the fiction I create didn't hold a candle to some of these true-life moments.

Remember, this is real. It happened, and there are thousands of others out there somewhere experiencing different degrees of this right now. If this book helps just one person realize that they aren't alone, Robin should feel incredibly proud.

Now it's your turn to read her brave story, and if you're anything like me, you'll want to jump onto the page and help. You'll be swearing at the words, because what you read will infuriate you. But, you'll also stop reading from time to time, letting the words sink in, feeling proud of how resilient this woman was.

Everyone's life is important, whether it be terrific or tragic, but it's what we do in those times, and how we react, that evolves us into who we are today. As you read Robin's story, you'll learn what happened in her younger years, but you'll also discover how she feels about everything today. Her words are blunt, courageous, and most importantly, honest. Robin doesn't hold back the punches. You'll see her encounter extreme lows, and you will follow her as she rises from those moments to become the wonderful, caring and inspirational woman she is today.

The brightest of lights are often born from the darkest shadows.

Robin, my friend, continues to shine.

Troy Barnes. Author of Deadlight, Monochromacy & The End of Ever.
troybarnes.com.au

Trail of Broken Hearts

As I walk along the trail of broken hearts, I see the littered souls of those who have gone before me, the shattered lives that were left behind, the sorrow, those who survived and managed to pick up the pieces and carry on, all the while burying the pain deep inside.

Alone are those who walk along the trail of broken hearts. Misery fills the air, and the gloom overcomes all who enter and walk amongst the lost souls. Death, despair, shattered vows, broken promises, lost innocence. Reasons to why this trail is littered so heavily with unhappy souls.

Dark clouds protrude from the sky and cast their spell down upon the aimless wanderers. Many tears have been shed along this treacherous path of shattered hopes and dreams. Some say the price of admission is too high and others are willing to forego the risk in hopes of finding the ultimate experience. In the land where promises are often tossed aside and forgotten, and where hopes and dreams are crushed, lost souls align and await our grand entrance.

Tragedy and grief lie deep within the oceans of our tears. Many ships drift on by as we immerse ourselves in our own sorrow. As I see the path of broken hearts trailing off in the distance, I turn back to look at all I have witnessed thus far. It's then that I realize that this was my own trail of broken hearts and tragedies that have impaled themselves upon me. As I turn back to look ahead, I take with me the knowledge that I have gained and now know that I can survive the trail of broken hearts.

Robin Y. Cotè

To help you in your journey, I have added five pages in the back where you can record your thoughts.

CHAPTER ONE

It all began when I was just thirteen years old. The day started out like any other day. I woke up, got dressed for school, ate breakfast, and headed out the door. There he was, sitting on the bench outside on the porch of my mom and dad's house. He had his legs outstretched, his arms crossed, and a rose in his mouth, with a slight smile on his face. He scared the hell out of me! "Good morning, sunshine," he said as he took the rose from his mouth and handed it to me. I recognized the voice. "How did you find me?" I asked him. He responded, "Oh, the other night while we were talking on the CB, I drove around in my car and tracked your signal. It wasn't hard to find you, since you guys had the only skyscraper antenna in the neighborhood. So, here I am!" I should have known at the time this wouldn't end well, but what the hell does any kid know at thirteen?

From the time I was seven years old, I had a fascination with talking on the CB radio. He was one of the people I had begun talking to just a few weeks before he showed up on my doorstep. I never gave him the impression I was interested in him. Hell, I was just a kid! He was four years older than I. I look back now and wonder why on earth he would go after a young girl who was only thirteen. At the time, I was charmed by him and didn't realize what was really going on.

He was sent to live here with his grandparents, because of the trouble he had gotten into back home in Indiana. We hung out a lot, talked and kissed. We spent hours on the phone at night. I was smitten. He knew it. I had just turned fourteen, and he was still hanging around. He began to pressure me for sex. I was scared to death and said no. He ended it. He didn't come around anymore or call. I was so devastated. Life went on.

His grandparents lived down the street from my Junior High, and I would pass by there on my way home every day. It was almost a year later when I decided to go by and say hi. I still felt something, but didn't know what it was. We rekindled our relationship, and it moved into a new direction. He began pressuring me to have sex with him when my parents were out of town. He refused to wear a condom, because he said they were uncomfortable. He told me to find some sort of birth control. I called my mom, asked her about birth control, and if I could take a friend of mine's. Of course she said no. She would take me to the doctor when they got back from their trip and get my own pills. I knew I had to solve this problem, or I would lose him. I was so naive back then.

He worked as a pizza delivery driver for Dominos at the time. He had a falling out with his grandparents, and they threw him out, so he claimed. He ended up sleeping in his car. He would douse himself with aftershave and take sponge baths in local restrooms. He would bring his laundry by our house, and I would help him out with it. My parents felt bad for him, and he managed to charm himself right into our home. My dad had closed off the garage to make an extra room. He and my brother shared that huge room, but that's not where he slept most of the time. He would sneak into my room at night and want to have sex. Yes, that happened more often than it should have. I didn't know what the hell I was doing. I just did what he said. I didn't want to disappoint him. I was a little scared of him and for good reason.

My parents were oblivious to what was beginning to happen. So was I at the time. The rules of the game had begun to change. I wasn't allowed to walk to school anymore. He had to drive me there. He would make sure what I wore was up to his standards. I wasn't allowed to show any skin, he said I couldn't. I developed a love for concert t-shirts, jeans and moccasins, which pretty much covered me up.

Things began to progress in the control area. There was a time when I tried to test this control he began to exhibit towards me. He said I couldn't wear a tank top and shorts, so I turned it around on him. "Then when you're outside washing your car, you have to keep your shirt on," I said. Of course he didn't like that and told me to fuck off. Nothing was accomplished. He still held the reigns tightly.

The power trip took a really bad turn when I expressed how I wanted to intern at another radio station again. I had done that when I was only eleven. I had a small part doing stuff with the morning show at a station, which was across the street and just slightly up the road from both my elementary and Jr. High school in Mesa.

It was the first time I witnessed something really ugly from him. He got within two inches of my face, yelled with spit and all. "Hell no! No woman of mine is going to go parading around with rock stars and fucking DJs." That gave me the scare of my life, but it was only the beginning of what I had to look forward to.

Every weekend, we would always go to the corner of Country Club and Southern to hang out at the 7-11. It was where everyone gathered to show off their vehicles and bullshit with each other. My brother was there most of the time and many of our friends as well. One night in particular really stands out in my memory. It was the first time he ever struck me, sort of. I was talking to one of our friends, when he came over and interrupted us. He grabbed my arm really hard and took me to the other side of the parking lot near T & D Furniture. At the time, this storefront had black iron bars on the windows. He yelled at me for talking to this person, and when I said I wasn't doing anything wrong, he took my head and slammed my face into the iron bars. I was lucky enough to turn my head slightly to avoid breaking my nose. The bars nailed my cheek and the bottom of my jaw. Nothing was broken, and no blood shed, but damn that hurt like hell! Several people, if not everyone, saw this, and no one did anything about it. No one said anything.

As I sit here and write this, recalling the memories, they are as vivid as if they just happened yesterday. My mind will not allow me to forget what I lived through, and my tears of anguish come flooding down. I don't want to relive this, but I have to. I can't be the victim. I can't allow him to make me his victim again. Not after 30 years.

CHAPTER TWO

You may wonder why I am choosing to relive all of this. I really have no choice in the matter. I am in my late 40s now, having lived through one of the most hellish times in my life, and I managed to survive. I lost a hell of a lot in the process, including a child, but I gained strength from it all. My strength is being tested yet again, as my previous hell is being thrown back at me, and someone is not telling the truth about it. The funny thing is, this former abuser of mine claims to be into God now. His latest wife got him into the church and something he calls "Fight Club." I believe this helps him deal with his anger issues...maybe? So much for being a church going lover of God. What a farce!

He is trying to do damage to a relationship, because he no longer has control over me. When an abuser, whether emotional, sexual or physical, loses control over their victim, they have nothing anymore. Once you learn to not fear them, they have no choice but to walk away, or find another way to inflict pain. Well, my former abuser has done just that and I can tell you, it HURTS LIKE HELL! I'm sure he knows it.

So, I must take back the power I gained in this horrible process and state the facts to clear up the lies. If the person this is meant for doesn't see the truth, then at least I can feel good knowing I don't have to keep the secrets I once did to protect my children. I will clarify more as I near the end of the story, and how all of this came to be. The TRUTH will be quite clear once all the evidence is shown, and the recent things said by my former abuser (in his own words) to both of my children, and God knows who else, will come to light.

I used to justify the abuse by saying he only hit me three times. Of course, that's three times too many! There are women who have suffered severe beatings, and some have even died from them. I was lucky, so I thought. I didn't realize the emotional abuse I endured was even worse. I would have preferred to be hit, because it would have been a wake-up call. Instead, I dealt with the emotional abuse almost daily and had no idea what I was enduring at the time. The scars he left me with are something I can certainly do without. There were so many things that happened that were warnings of what was to come. I had no idea. I was so naive and vulnerable back then.

One of the very first things that happened in our relationship should have clued me in to his control issues. Most of us love the idea of getting our first car and having the freedom of being able to drive ourselves around. I wasn't so lucky with that experience. At the time, he drove an older Datsun 510. He came up with this great idea of having matching his and her cars. I thought it would be cool, and it made me feel like he really wanted to display his feelings for me. I couldn't have been more wrong. I ended up buying an orange 510 he had found in the classifieds. It sat for the longest time, and never got fixed up. He didn't bother messing with it, other than stripping parts off of it to fix up his own car. So much for having my own car to drive. What a fucked up thing to do to me, and all in the name of love.

Another incident comes to mind as I sit here reliving this shadow of my former life. Something set him off one day. We were lying back on my bed, halfway up on the pillows. He was pissed at me. I can't recall what for. My mind goes numb from time to time on some of the details. I guess it's our brains way of protecting us. Too bad it didn't wipe out what came next. He had a small pistol at the time. I can see it in my mind so clearly as if I'm watching a movie. He put that gun to my head and threatened to blow a hole in me. I was terrified! Why would he do this to me? I was always being threatened with this "If you say anything" shit. I felt so alone. He had everyone in my family snowed. How could they not see through him? If I wasn't in school, I had to be with him or at home and not out with friends. In fact, I really had no friends anymore.

Strike number two came out of the blue. We were driving around, and I brought up wanting to hang out with my friend Lora. He didn't want to hear anything about it. I raised my voice slightly, and I paid for it. He slapped me across the face. I was in shock, and I couldn't believe what had just happened. I threw open the door and jumped out of the moving car at the corner of Extension and 8th Avenue in Mesa. He screamed at me and sped off. I had no idea where he was going, or what he was going to do to me next.

I was stunned and in a daze. I never left that corner. I was holding my face and crying for what seemed like an eternity. He came back and pulled up to the curb. I noticed he had my mother in the car with him. Not what I was expecting at all. She told me to get in the car and go home with them. I tried to explain what just happened, but she told me to stop crying, quit acting like a kid, and get in the car. This was MY mom! The one who loved me, my ultimate protector. She had no idea what had just happened. That son of a bitch had her fooled! Now you understand why I felt so damn helpless and felt like I could never go to anyone with what was happening. I didn't even understand it myself! I was only 15!

In my mom's defense, she has no recall of this event, and I can't blame her for anything. It's not her fault that I brought a sociopath into our lives. Yes, that is what he is, A SOCIOPATH. Sociopaths have little regard for the feelings of others and manipulate others in order to get what they desire. The term "sociopath" is no longer used in psychology and psychiatry, and the disorder is now called "antisocial personality disorder." People who have this disorder often have no sense of right or wrong.

I didn't have a clue of this until about 15 years ago, when I met a shrink and was discussing this past life. He said to me, "My God, did you realize that you had married a sociopath? You are lucky to be alive." You're telling me! The shrink even called him a child predator. I remember when I first started to get to know his grandparents. His grandmother Marilyn told me one time that a "chemical imbalance" ran on that side of the family. They all believed he had that problem, because he had issues with his temper. He often argued with his old-school grandfather Ben. I saw this happen a few times. I was clueless that there was anything to it other than a teenager and his older relative not agreeing on how things were to be done.

As time progressed, the emotional torment continued. This may get a bit graphic, but it needs to be said. One day he accused me of lying about being a virgin when I slept with him the first time. I remember my first time having sex very well, and it most definitely was with him in the backseat of his fucking little car. He got into an argument with my mother over it. She came to my defense, and I couldn't have been happier. He said, "I didn't bust her cherry, so I know she's fucking lying about being a virgin." Yes, those were his exact words! My mom went on to explain that, when I was 10 years old, I had been in an accident. At the time, we were living off of Center and McLellan, just north of Hohokam Ballpark.

I was riding my bike home, and a lady veered into the bike lane, hitting me and knocking me off into the roadway. I had some scrapes, road rash and bruises. I got pretty lucky, but something else happened that day. I was bleeding from my pubic area. The doctor checked me out: there was no serious damage done, and no internal bleeding that was serious in nature. Apparently, the bleeding was the so-called cherry that you men boast about breaking in women who are virgins. What the hell did I know? I was only 10 when that happened. I didn't realize five-and-a-half years later it would be held against me that I didn't have a damn cherry to burst.

My hell wasn't quite over yet, although I was about to get a reprieve. School was somewhat of an escape for me. It was my time to be away from him, even though I had to be taken to school, met at lunch most of the time and picked up at the end of the day. I lost myself in my studies and was an A and B student. He let me hang around with one friend, and he even liked her. That was Karen. I wasn't sure at the time why, but it came to light later on. She was living with an older guy who worked maintenance for the public school system.

My ex, Karen and I went to see Journey in concert together. You can imagine how thrilled I was to be able to have her there with us. My ex even brought liquor to her and me during our lunch break from time to time. I was afraid to drink at school, but Karen said we could mix some JD in with our coke, and no one would know it since we had PE right after lunch. I couldn't understand why I was finally allowed to have a friend.

It wasn't long after this that he decided to break up with me. It was during my senior year, sometime in October. I was heartbroken. Don't ask me why. I should have been happy. All of a sudden, my grades began dropping, and I couldn't concentrate in class. I was so lost. I thought it was because of the break-up. I couldn't have been more wrong. I tried my hardest to move beyond it all, but it wasn't easy. My whole life was about to change, and I didn't even know it yet.

I began ditching my morning classes and hanging out at one of the radio stations here in town. I had met and become friends with one of the DJs who had just gotten an overnight gig there. Not long after that, he managed to score the morning show. Over time, I ended up becoming good friends with several of the people connected to the show, one in particular who became like a big brother to me, Jeff. The whole morning crew was so nice, and it eventually led me into an internship at the station.

In early November, I got called into the Assistant Principals office. I remember it like it was yesterday. She told me I was failing my classes. She couldn't understand what had happened to one of her best students. Hell, I didn't even know. She gave me two options: either drop out, or we kick you out. Some option, huh? I'm out either way. Neither looks good on your record. So, I dropped out. The following week was my 17th birthday. I decided to go to the local college and apply to get my GED. I passed the test with flying colors!

I still felt weird inside, like something wasn't quite right. I felt very alone. I thought maybe I was feeling down due to the whole school thing, or because of my relationship with Mike ending. I began the process of looking into career choices and schooling, which helped get my mind off of things.

I met a couple, Ray and Kim, and started hanging out with them. They were cool people, and they helped get me out of the funk I was in. They sort of adopted me as their little sister. They invited me to go with them to a Christmas party at the Haystack apartments, off of Dobson and Baseline. They introduced me to a neighbor of their friend. His name was Steve. I had a great time talking to everyone and being out and about for a change of scenery. Little did I know, things were about to take a very bad turn that night.

Steve brought me over a glass of beer. I wasn't old enough to legally drink yet, but decided that just a little sip wouldn't hurt. Big mistake! I don't remember a damn thing until I woke up, and it wasn't pretty! I had something stuffed in my mouth, my hands were tied back, and my clothes were in a pile on the floor. What the hell was going on? This big guy was on top of me. He was crushing all of his weight down onto me. I realized that I was on a weight lifting bench. I couldn't move. I began to struggle and tried to scream, but my voice was muffled. I looked around to see where the hell I was. The door was closed. It was a bedroom. I saw a prosthetic leg up against the wall. I noticed the guy on top of me only had one leg and a stump near the midpoint of his thigh on the other. I wanted to puke. Who the hell was this guy, and why was he doing this to me?

Tears were streaming down my hot face, mascara burning my eyes, snot running out of my nose and down my cheeks. I was gasping for air as he thrust his huge body into mine, crushing my chest and stomach. *I've got to get out of this hell! I've got to fight this!* I struggled so much that he finally fell off of me and hit the floor. I don't know how I was able to free my hands, but I did. I got up and ran into him, knocking him down as he was trying to get up. It was Steve! I grabbed my stuff and yanked open the door. I ran toward the next room looking for an exit. Much to my surprise, I saw a woman around 40 or so, and another much older woman sitting there watching TV. I screamed at them. "What the hell is the matter with you? He just raped me and you didn't do a fucking thing about it!" They just stared at me, not saying a word, so I got the hell out of there.

I ran down the stairs as fast as I could, tripping several times and skinning my knees on the steps. I was screaming in the parking lot. Ray and Kim came outside and quickly took me to their truck. Someone brought over a blanket and wrapped it around me. I couldn't say anything. I was numb. I don't remember anything after that. I don't even remember how I got home.

I crawled into a shell for the next five weeks. I was so confused. I just wanted to get the hell out of here. I wanted to disappear. I don't really remember how I made it through each day at that point. I did however, make a decision that would have changed my life, had it worked out. I decided I needed a fresh start. I went down to the local military recruiting place to see about joining the service. I started working on a plan, but it wasn't meant to be. They had me do a standard piss test and then I got the news. "You can't join the military because you are pregnant." WHAT?

CHAPTER THREE

It's never an easy process to relive things from your past, but those things are what led to me being who I am today. I am no longer a victim, and writing is my greatest strength. I'm not bitter. I'm not angry. I'm not vengeful. I'm just a survivor who has a story to tell.

There are others who have undergone worse and are not around to tell the tale. I was lucky enough to survive and become a much better person. I take responsibility for my share of things. No one is perfect. I will tell the truth no matter what happens. No matter what it costs me. It has already cost me a lot, but that's okay. I've learned to live with it and make changes for the better.

Not everyone grows up in the best environment. We can't pick our families. We are born into them. My former abuser grew up in a household that had some major issues. Alcohol and anger don't mix, especially when you have three children to raise. I'm sure the abuse he suffered played a major part in who he became as an adult, but that doesn't excuse him from his actions as an adult. He could have gotten the help he needed and broken the cycle. I did see the good in him from time to time, but then the ugliness would surface, and the good would disappear. I truly believe anyone can change if they really want to. I would have hoped this was the case for my former abuser, but it wasn't, and probably never will be.

If he had changed, then he would have told the truth, no matter how ugly it was. We were both to blame for things. I was too young to know any better most of the time. I'm sure my upbringing played a major role in this as well. I had a wonderful mother who did anything for her kids. We were her world. That's why it amazed me that he was able to get to her, and she chose to believe him over me.

My father was there for us by putting the roof over our heads and clothes on our backs. Yes, he told us he loved us and hugged us while we were growing up, but he wasn't the dream father people thought he was. He took a lot out on my mother that he shouldn't have. He was very bitter about his first marriage, and he carried that into his relationship with my mother. Many don't know these things about him, and it's going to get uglier as I go along in the story.

He complained so often through the years that he worked hard for his money, yet his first wife would never let him have his paycheck. He said that no one was going to have that kind of control over him ever again. He made sure my mother would never be an independent woman. He always took her money she made working outside of the home as a nanny. She was never allowed to learn how to drive, and the kicker to this...he used to scare the hell out of her about learning to drive. My brother and I tried many times to encourage her to learn, and we offered to teach her, but she wouldn't do it.

My dad had six children from his previous marriage. Over time, several of those children have said, if their parents had stayed together, they would have all become successful doctors and lawyers. I wish this were true for them. Some of them think my brother and I are successful because of our parents, especially because of our dad. Not the case. Like I said, this is going to get brutal before it gets better.

My dad never encouraged us to do anything. He would always find the cheap way out. I developed major dental issues as an adult, because my father didn't do right by me as a child when it came to proper dental care. My brother and I so wanted a dad who would do things with us while we were growing up. He wasn't that kind of father. Sure, we had a pool table in the family room, and he would shoot pool with us on occasion, but did he ever go outside and play catch with my brother? No. Did he ever support us wanting to do Boy/Girl Scouts or after school sports? Hell no. Would he drive us places? Nope.

My dad was 40 years old when I was born. My memories of my childhood are as follows: he would come home from working at the post office, nap on the couch, eat dinner, and watch *Lawrence Welk*, *Little House on the Prairie*, *Donny and Marie*, *Cher*, *Bonanza*, *The Rifleman*, The *Waltons*, etc. You get it. My fondest memory is when he would rub my back as I laid in bed and tell me goodnight. At least we got some love from him. It wasn't enough. We wanted more from him, but it wasn't meant to be. Maybe it was a product of his upbringing. He was one of ten children growing up on a farm in Canada.

On his time off, my father would go into the garage and always be tinkering with stuff. He did typewriter repairs and then went on to become a locksmith. Spending time with us was not an option. If he didn't want kids, why the hell did he have eight of us? I'm sure he would say something to defend his actions, but my brother and I lived it. We know how things went down. He would certainly never win the father of the year award.

I'm not bitter about it. I've learned to get over it. What that experience did for me was to make me try even harder not to be that kind of parent to my own child. I never wanted my child to feel as if I didn't believe in him. Dreams are important, and sometimes sacrifices have to be made in order to survive, but you can't ever stop believing in your dreams, or you die inside. This was what I would make sure to pass on to my child, no matter what. And that brings me back to the beginning again: finding out I was pregnant.

Pregnant? How could that be? I'm on birth control. Then it hit me. Oh God, this kid is a product of the rape! I had heard things about alcohol affecting the birth control pill, making it null and void. That scared the hell out of me! How on earth was I going to deal with this? I wasn't about to have a child that was a result of such a brutal act. I know I would deprive that child of a good life, because all I would do is look at him and think of the rape. I could never get past that.

I decided to take a second test to make sure I was in fact pregnant. I went to the Planned Parenthood clinic down the street from my old high school. They did a free pregnancy test for me and again, the results were positive. With this information, I now faced a really tough thing, telling my parents and disappointing them.

My mom was very understanding. I told them about the rape. I thought my dad would have been outraged and on the hunt to find Steve. That didn't happen. In fact, I don't remember much emotion from him at all. I showed them the paperwork I had been given from Planned Parenthood that listed the different options available to me. I told them I wanted to get an abortion, because I would not bring a child into this world that was a product of rape. I know I'm going to catch some hell for writing this, because some people believe that every child deserves a chance to live. Sure they do, BUT it's MY CHOICE not to bring an unwanted child into this world: a child who was not made out of love, but was conceived in an act of violence against a woman.

So I called and scheduled the abortion. My father drove me down to the Planned Parenthood office. Yes, they actually performed some abortions in their offices back then. I was scared to death! This wasn't over yet, and at the time, I didn't think it ever would be. The doctor was a much older man, around 50 or so, grey hair, glasses, green eyes, wrinkles around his eyes and cheeks, and a very well-worn look on his face I remember so well. I'm sure it wasn't easy for him being thought of as a baby killer. The nurse was off to the side, ready to aide him in whatever he needed. The doctor had to do an ultrasound to determine the exact age of the fetus. I was terrified!

Next he wanted to do a pelvic exam. I didn't understand the reasoning behind all this. I thought the tube would be inserted and the fetus would be sucked out. Game over, move on somehow, and try to forget this nightmare. Let me tell you something. You don't know shit at 17!

He told me to relax, and it felt as if I were being raped and violated all over again. I wanted to scream, "Get your fucking hands off of me and out of me!" I tried to hold back the tears, but I couldn't. I despise pelvic exams!

Then it was over. Or was it? He stopped everything he was doing, left me there spread eagle in stirrups, and had a consult with the nurse. I became hysterical. I didn't know what the hell was going on. I shouldn't have been left like that for what seemed a lifetime.

They finally came back over to me. The words are still so strong in my memory, and I can hear the doctor's voice as if he were standing here talking to me now. "We are not going to be able to perform a standard abortion on you today. We're going to let you get dressed, and the nurse is going to talk to you about some alternative options."

WHAT? Alternative options? What the hell are you talking about? I was not getting dressed and leaving that room. I was not going to continue to carry this child, this product of rape inside my body. I wanted to know what the hell was going on, and I was going to find out RIGHT NOW!

The nurse tried to calm me down. The doctor then proceeded to tell me, "We can't do a routine abortion on you, because you are 4 1/2 months pregnant. That would require a partial term abortion, and we don't perform those in this office."

Four-and-a-half months pregnant? How could this be? Again, I questioned this, because I was on birth control. There had only been two men I had been sexual with: my abuser and the guy who raped me. I was raped in December. The timeline didn't fit with the rapist being the father of the baby.

CHAPTER FOUR

Those words echoed in my head over and over: four-and-a-half months pregnant, four-and-a-half months pregnant. How could that be? I was on birth control and was still having my period. Doesn't that stop when you are pregnant? Talk about having a brick shit house leveled on me at that moment. I was so prepared to end the life of a fetus, who was the product of a violent incident in my life. It wasn't easy to come to that decision. I'm not a killer. I had no choice in the matter. BUT THIS? I was not expecting this! Four-and-a-half months pregnant, four-and-a-half months pregnant. His words echoed in my head. This wasn't happening...but yes it was.

I was numb. I had a lot to think about. The game plan needed to change. I didn't sleep at all that night. The next day, I decided to take a drive up to my usual quiet spot overlooking the city. We called it Microwave Mountain. I hiked up the mountainside and sat upon a rock overlooking the valley. I sat up there for what seemed an eternity. I cried and cried. I sat silent at times. I closed my eyes and let the wind try to carry my thoughts away and ease my heaviness.

A cool breeze began to filter past me, bringing a tingling sensation over my body. I looked up and noticed storm clouds approaching from the distance. The sun was barely peeking out as the clouds began to form overhead. It seemed so quiet now, like there was nothing else in existence except for myself. I cried out several times, as if I were hoping someone had the answers for me.

All of a sudden, as if out of nowhere, in the still quiet surroundings, a little sparrow landed beside the rock I was sitting on. He began to move closer, and I tried to scare him away with a swish of my hand, but he wouldn't budge. He continued his jaunt over to me and suddenly flew up to my leg, landing there, catching me by surprise. He gazed up at me and just sat there with a bewildered look upon his little face. He continued to wander up my leg, not breaking his stare for one moment. He stopped, and then began to let out a few chirps, as if to tell me something. I reached down, and to my amazement; he jumped onto the palm of my hand. I began to stroke his feathers as he sang cheerfully. I felt a calming peace come over me. A few moments later, he bolted out of my hand and took off in flight. He was gone. As I sat upon that rock on that lonely mountainside, I wondered what could have possessed this little bird to do such a crazy thing. It was then I realized I had gotten my sign, and I knew what I had to do.

I told my parents I planned on keeping the baby, since it had been conceived out of love and not during an act of violence. In my mind, it was love, but what the hell did I know? I was just a kid myself when all this happened. My life was about to change in ways I'd never imagined. Some of it good, some of it a nightmare I'm still dealing with to this day.

I am a good person. I believed the right thing to do at the time was contact my ex and let him know I was pregnant with his child. I called his grandparents to locate him, and they gave me his address. He was living in a small apartment complex up on Main St. behind a high performance shop. I told him I didn't expect anything, or want anything from him, I just thought he should know about the baby.

He decided he wanted to reconcile and work things out. I wasn't expecting that. It became evident pretty quickly why he wanted to get back together. It was all about the sex. He wanted to have sex, and he felt we were safe since I was pregnant. He never expressed any excitement about becoming a parent. What guy at 21 wants a kid, right? I just wanted to give my baby his/her father. I wasn't thinking about anything else.

During our time of reconciliation, I wanted to do something special for him. Since he wanted me to spend time with him at his place, I felt the need to clean it up. It was pretty disgusting to be honest. I can see the layout in my mind right now, as if I'm in that apartment today. The sink was full of water, dirty dishes, live and dead cockroaches. YUCK! I almost puked many times as I put my hands in that water. Several of the cockroaches would crawl up my hands. It sends chills down my spine to this day to remember it.

This next part kind of makes me laugh, but cringe at the same time. He had a thing for waterbeds. He didn't put his sheets on the bed like normal people do. The blue mattress was always exposed, and the sheets lay crumpled off in the corner. When I decided to make the bed, I saw, and I kid you not, about a dozen cockroaches on top of the mattress. They looked like they were ice skating across the top. See, I told you it was kind of funny, but gross.

Over the next few weeks, things seemed to be going well. No arguing, no control being exhibited – smooth sailing, but it didn't last.

His friend John called me and said he needed to talk to me about Mike and the baby. I didn't know what was going on, but I told him I would come by later that day. This was his best friend at the time, so I thought it must have been important. I couldn't have been more wrong.

John lived in a duplex right on Extension facing the roadway, across the street from my old junior high school. When I got there, I found a note on the door that said to come in. I called out to him several times when I walked inside, but got no answer. He then came down the hallway wearing nothing but a towel around his waist. I didn't really think anything of it at first, but, I was so naive.

I asked him what was going on, and what was so important he needed to talk to me about. He touched my arm lightly as he expressed his feelings to me. He said Mike was no good for me. He wanted to be with me, take care of me and the baby. He touched my face, pulled me close to him and tried to kiss me. What the fuck! I pushed him away from me. "What the hell are you doing? You're his best friend! This is his baby! I love him! How dare you do this to me! What is wrong with you?"

I ran out of there as fast as I could. My face was on fire, and tears were streaming down my cheeks. How in the hell could John do this to me? Why would he try to take me away from his best friend? Why now, when I am carrying his best friend's child? Why weren't there signs of this in the past? Why didn't he express these feelings when Mike and I were broken up? I honestly felt like he was full of shit. I got the feeling it was all about wanting to have sex with me, and not so much about wanting to be with me for the future. I'm pretty sure I was right. Can't knock up a girl and be blamed for it when you already know she's preggo, right?

I just wanted to forget about what happened with John. After being raped by Steve, I sure as hell didn't want to be in that situation again. It almost felt like it when John tried to force that kiss on me. I was too afraid to tell Mike about what John did. I was worried it would destroy their friendship and cause problems in our relationship. I didn't want that for our baby. I sometimes feel like I should have told Mike, but then again, would he have even believed me? Knowing who he is now, and the things we did go through, would he have blamed me for the incident? I can hear the words right now in my mind, "You went over there, so you must have come on to him. It's your fault that shit happened to you."

So, I kept it quiet for the most part. I should have told someone other than Karen. She was supposed to be my best friend, but I learned later on, she really wasn't. It's hard enough to trust people, especially with your deepest darkest secrets, but when they betray you; that can almost destroy you. She is the reason why I never trusted most women throughout my life. You will come to understand why later in the story.

Within weeks of our reconciliation, it was over. Mike ended it. He said he didn't want to be together and that, "he didn't want no damn kid!" I should have seen this coming. Since the incident with John, Mike had been acting strange. I wondered if John had said something to him. You bet your ass he did. I didn't know this at the time, but I had a feeling something had been said.

I was devastated. Here I was alone and pregnant. No military to whisk me away from this god forsaken hell, no father for my kid, lost and feeling helpless. What was I going to do? I had to stop thinking like that. I did the right thing by telling this man he had a child on the way. He made the decision to walk away. Now I had to prepare myself to undertake the challenge of a lifetime; being a single parent to this child. Was I scared? Hell yes! I was terrified!

I threw myself into the internship at the radio station. I was working part-time as well. I didn't want to think about what I was going to do, I just did it. I tried to stay as positive as I could, but it wasn't easy. The best thing I had going for me at the time was my mother. She was actually looking forward to the baby being born. Mom and dad would volunteer at their church every Sunday. Dad was the usher, and mom would take care of the babies and toddlers in the nursery. This gave her access to things I wasn't able to afford and my dad was too cheap to buy, like a crib and playpen.

I felt bad that I was still living at home and about to have a baby. I was only 17, so what could I do? Mom and I turned my brother's old room into a nursery. It's kind of strange when I think back on it now. That was the room I used to sneak into when I was younger to talk on the CB. My fascination with that damn squawk box is what got me into this trouble to begin with.

CHAPTER FIVE

Time was passing by so quickly now. So much to get ready for, but not quite sure I was prepared for it. Are we ever prepared to become parents, especially at 17? Hell no, but what choice did I have? I made the decision to keep this baby, and I was going to do whatever I had to for this kid.

My life was now in his hands, as I made him a promise while he lay curled up inside my belly. "You will always be the most important thing in my life. I will never make you feel unwanted. I will shower you with all the love you are meant to have. I will strive to be the best I can be, so you will never have to worry about not having a father in your life. I'm proud to be your mother, and I will never let you down. I will make sure you will be proud to have me as your mother."

I came up with his name, Jeffrey Michael. I chose the name Jeffrey to honor my dear friend who was there for me as a big brother. I wanted my son to have his father's name as his middle name, even though his father had chosen to not be in his life. It still meant something to me to give him his name, and it had a nice ring to it.

I thought either Lora or Karen would have surprised me with a baby shower, but that didn't happen. Lora had been a childhood friend who had dropped out of high school in 10th grade to get married. She distanced herself from most of her friends after that. If she had stayed in school, I'm sure Karen and I would not have become best friends.

It's amazing how you think the two people you consider as best friends, even sisters at times, would do something for you as simple as a baby shower, but they didn't bother. I can't blame Lora, since she was wrapped up in her own marriage, which apparently had major issues. I thought Karen would do something, since she had lots of free time. I was visiting her one day and was tempted to bring it up. Something stopped me dead in my tracks and forever changed, not only my relationship with her, but my ability to trust women in general.

A shiny gold bracelet caught my eye as the light in the room reflected off of it. I saw a glimpse of the name that was etched into the top of it. Can you guess what it was? Michael. You could say I was more than a little shocked at this. I knew her pretty well at the time, or so I thought. She never mentioned she was involved with anyone other than Ralph. He took care of her. Why would she risk screwing around with anyone else and lose the best thing she had going?

I remember grabbing her wrist and pulling the bracelet closer to my face so I could verify what I had seen. Yep, there it was: Michael. She yanked her arm away and turned her back to me. The room had just taken on a really icy feel. What the hell was going on here? Was she cheating on Ralph? Why would she be wearing a bracelet with another man's name on it and still be living in Ralph's house? It was a lot worse than I thought. The shit was about to hit the fan!

I questioned her. She let me know she had been seeing someone else and sleeping with them for the past six months. She said Ralph had no problem with it, and she could still live there with him if she wanted to. Okay, but that's a little weird, don't you think? When I asked who Michael was, she clammed up, and once again turned her back on me so I couldn't see her face. I knew something wasn't right with this whole thing. I had a horrible pain deep down in my chest. I didn't want to believe it. Could she have been sleeping with my Michael? Could she have been screwing around with my child's father?

I had to know, so I just said it. "Is it my Michael who you've been sleeping with?" She didn't say anything, which pretty much told me the answer. I started to cry, and it wasn't pretty what came next. "You fucking bitch! How could you do this to me and my baby? You knew we were trying to work it out, and yet you were fucking him at the same time!"

I was dealt a harsh blow that day. I guess I finally got the answer I was looking for from so long ago as to why I was allowed to have her as a friend. He had his eye on her for a long time. I had lost my best friend that day. I actually lost her a long time before then, and I didn't even know it. Damn her! Damn him! Fuck the both of them! I walked out that door and out of her life for good.

CHAPTER SIX

Since I started writing this book, I've had many comments, messages and phone calls from people. Some I've never met; some I've known half my life: former bosses, co-workers and friends. I'm amazed at the feedback I've been getting, and I can't thank you all enough. It's not an easy journey, as I've stated before. I've already lived it and still do to some extent today.

Many of you have expressed concern for what my ex-abuser may do to me if he finds out about me going public with all of this. I am no longer afraid of him. This is why he has chosen to strike back at me through my children. It's not fair to them. It's certainly not fair to me. I never believed in sharing every dirty, filthy, horrible detail with them. I only told the truth of what led to certain things. I never spoke badly about him to my son while he was growing up. I knew better than that. It was up to him to inquire about details when he was old enough to understand.

You need not worry about what my ex will do to me. He won't show his face at my door. That's not his style. If he happens to do that, I would defend myself. I do own a gun, and I'm very good with it when need be. I would most likely use my own hands, since I am pretty strong, and I don't take anyone's shit anymore. I don't like violence, but I'll be damned if it's going to be me dead at his hands!

His approach would be something more of a sneaky nature. He might shoot me from afar. He might slash my car tires. He slashed all four of the tires on my Nova a long time ago after we broke up. He may even drive by and throw a brick through my window. It's hard to say if he would even bother coming here, although he does savor confrontation between himself and a woman. He doesn't fight men. He only hits, belittles and manipulates women and children. That's more his style.

If in fact he does return to Arizona to cause problems, his second ex-wife has assured me that local law enforcement will handle the situation. If something should by chance happen to me, well then this will serve as a record to who the authorities should look at first. I have studied forensics to a certain degree. I have worked with the police, lawyers and the attorney general's office before. I know the order of a crime investigation. Almost everyone in my life from back then is still alive and can testify as to what transpired, the threats that were made a few years back and all the things said now. With this being said in writing, they will most certainly go to him first as a suspect. Enough said. It's time to get back to the story.

As I began the eighth month of my pregnancy, I received a phone call. It was Mike. He wanted to come over and talk to me. I had no idea what to expect. He did sound sincere on the phone, but this is Mike we are talking about. He could charm the pants off of anyone. I only wish I had known that at the time.

My heart, tainted by my pregnancy hormones, made me reluctantly agree to meet him. He came by that night, and we sat outside and talked. He said he had been thinking about things and wanted to get back together, get married and have this kid. I was kind of dumbfounded. Why the change of heart all of a sudden? I just had to ask, "Why now? You said all those horrible things to me when you broke it off last time."

He told me John had put him up to it. John told him that he shouldn't be saddled with some stupid bitch and her damn baby. Wow! Did John also happen to mention the incident that happened at his apartment the last time we saw each other? Did he tell him he tried to kiss me and wanted to have sex with me? I don't know, since Mike never brought it up.

Apparently they had a falling out, and he decided he wanted to work it out with me. He never told me what actually happened with John, and at that point, I really didn't care. I was only thinking about being able to give my child his father, and I wasn't going to have to do this alone. I didn't even think about the whole Karen mess either. Honestly, what the hell was wrong with me? I should have gone full bore on his ass about him cheating on me with my best friend while we were reconciling the last time. As usual, he had gotten to me. I was blinded by his charm.

He seemed genuine when he started talking about marriage. I was having doubts about his sincerity, so I had a stipulation. I said I would give him another chance, but wouldn't marry him until after the baby was born. I wanted to wait just to make sure. He reluctantly agreed. What choice did he really have? Marrying him was one thing he couldn't force me to do. I had to be willing to do it.

CHAPTER SEVEN

Being a small business owner gives me the opportunity to meet people from all walks of life. Sometimes when we go to do an estimate, we end up socially talking with our potential clients. I'm amazed at how some of these discussions turn extremely personal, and they share memories of their past, not always pleasant. Today I had that experience. I met an incredible woman with a story to share. It was a story that ran along the same lines as the one I've been sharing with you. Some of her details varied from mine, but the end result was the same. She was abused, both physically and emotionally, by her first husband, and she somehow managed to get out alive.

Her name is Donna. My husband Joe and I began talking to her and her boyfriend Tim about the job they wanted us to do. Within a short amount of time, we started talking about her rescued dogs and my rescuing birds. As Tim and Joe began talking about cars, she went on to tell me about how rough she had it in her previous life, and that helping these two rescue dogs was also helping her. Her twins were now 38 years old. She is now in her 60s. They were the children tied to her first husband and the really bad experiences she went through.

She described the relationship and the things she and the children endured for many years because of this man. His rage and behavior was fueled by alcohol and a need to control her. She was staring off in the distance as she told me the details. The tears began welling up in her eyes.

You could see the movie playing out in her mind as she filled in the details. The twins were part of the abuse, and yet the father tried to manipulate them years later, by saying their mother had lied to them. She never spoke a bad word about their father to them. She kept a lot of the details quiet. They stood up to their father and said he couldn't lie, because they were there, and they remembered everything. They were 14 when their father left them.

Why did he leave? I knew what she was going to say, and when she did, I could feel the tears welling up in my own eyes. He left the day after she stood up to him, just like my situation. He had lost the power, and she had gained the strength she needed to protect herself and her children. She leaned forward and whispered the words she said to him that day when he threatened to hurt their children. "You've fucked with me long enough. If you fuck with them, I will do everything in my power to kill you."

I had met another survivor of this brutal war. I didn't even mention my situation, or that I was writing this book, until she shared these details with me. I am more determined than ever to finish this and get it out there. It amazes me that this problem exists on such a vast scale, and yet so many people are afraid to open themselves up and get their stories out there. I don't mind being the mouth piece for them as well as myself.

Love is a very special thing, and for people to come along in our lives and taint love with their skewed view of what it should be, is just not right. Children should never be used as our personal pin cushions or punching bags. We should always take special care of the relationships we build with them, so they become well-adjusted, healthy adults. There is enough hate and crap to deal with in life as it is. Now let's get back to my story.

Right after the reconciliation, we got a little bit of bad news. The baby was in a breach position. His head was underneath my ribs, legs, underneath the other ribs, and his butt was smack dab over the birth canal. They scared the hell out of me when they tried to turn him. My stomach turned bright blue and he just wouldn't budge. So they made the decision to take him by caesarean once the time had come.

Three weeks later, I went into labor. I called my doctor, and he asked me to stay at home until they called me to come in to the hospital. I couldn't understand this, since they knew I was having a C-section done. I was in labor for over 30 hours before the call came. I was in labor another six hours before I was on the table ready to have the baby.

In the delivery room, I was surrounded by several doctors and nurses, the anesthesiologist and Mike. They hung a sheet across my mid-section, and I could no longer see my stomach. I was so scared at that moment. Why wasn't I allowed to see what was going on? I was given the drugs to numb me, and then it was time for the baby to be born. I remember feeling the scalpel cut into me, and then I didn't feel anything anymore. I heard the baby cry a short time later. Jeffrey Michael was now here. At that instant, I knew my life was going to be different. I didn't feel like a 17-year-old kid anymore. I felt like a mama bear ready to protect her cub.

The nurse took the baby and cleaned him up. Before they started sewing and stapling me up, a group of over 20 young people in white jackets came into the room and filled up all the empty spaces. I had no idea what was going on, but I was about to find out. The doctor talked to the group about something rare in women. He pointed out that I had a dual chambered uterus. So here I was: I had just gone through 36 hours of labor, had a C-section, and my entire insides were on display to a group of medical students. Talk about awkward!

Both Jeffrey and I were released from the hospital after five days. I could barely move. I felt like I had been hit by a Mack truck! Not an easy thing to have half of your body torn open, sewn and stapled shut. My mom did quite a few things for me when I got back home, since I was having a rough time getting back on my feet. I don't have any recall of Mike doing anything for the baby, or having any type of emotion. I can't really remember anything that stands out.

Things seemed to be going okay with Mike, and he was now working with my brother at a lumber yard. I began to think the baby had changed him, and I was never going to see that ugly side of him ever again. At least I was hoping the beast wouldn't return. I was trying to plan the wedding, and dealing with being a new mom, all at the same time. I couldn't plan anything too fancy or big, due to financial reasons, so we planned a small ceremony at Pioneer Park in Mesa. We planned an October 12th wedding, which was just a couple of months away.

The month of August was the beginning of a whole new set of nightmares for our family. We should have been celebrating new life in the house and my parent's upcoming wedding anniversary, but that was all tainted by the accident that happened at the lumber yard. My brother had all of the fingers on his left hand ripped off by a table saw, not the kind of thing you would expect to happen. This tore my mother up, and she had a tough time watching her son go through all the pain he had to endure. No one wants to see their child go through that kind of trauma.

With everything that was going on at the time, I had no idea of the shit storm that was about to land on my doorstep and rip at my heart. Here I was, alone at home with my baby. The doorbell rang. It was a woman holding a small infant in her arms. The baby was dressed in pink, so I assumed it was a girl. I had never seen this woman before. She asked if Mike was home. Umm, no, he didn't live here. Why was she looking for him, and who was she?

She mentioned his grandmother told her he would most likely be at my home. Okay, so who are you and what do you want with Mike? I asked her several times, but she was reluctant to answer. She then asked me who I was, and why I was interested as to her business with him. I told her we were engaged to be married, and we just had a son in July. I don't think that was quite the answer she was expecting, as things turned a little nasty in her tone.

"Oh, really? I'M the mother of his child, and he needs to sign her birth certificate," she said as she shoved her arms forward at me with the baby and document in hand. What the hell was she talking about? I wasn't sure what to think. She then went on to tell me her name was Debbie, and her brother John was his best friend. Ah okay, so now the shit comes full circle. John probably put her up to this, for one last ditch attempt at messing with us, since he and Mike had a falling out. I told her I had no idea what the hell she was talking about, since they ended their friendship. She just laughed at me and said, "You better tell him to contact me so we can take care of this!" She turned and left.

Later that day, I called Mike and asked him to come over, because we needed to talk. I admit, I was more than a little upset with this latest thing. I had been waiting for the other shoe to drop, and it finally did. It's one of the reasons why I wanted to wait to get married and not rush into it. He told me he had screwed around with John's sister Debbie a few times, but the baby was not his. He claimed she was a prostitute, and that he had lived with her for a short time at a motel in Phoenix. Once he found out she was hooking, he dumped her.

This guy was pretty busy in between all of our breakups and reconciliations. Not only did he screw my best friend, but he hooked up with a supposed prostitute too. I should have seen the warning signs in all of this, but again, he charmed me. He seemed sincere in his explanation of things, so I didn't doubt him. I was so damn naive!

CHAPTER EIGHT

This past Sunday started like any of our normal off-roading days. I was looking forward to this one more than anything. This particular trail starts in the desert and works its way through the mountains until you reach the forest. A huge drop in temperature this time of year, and the scenery is awesome! I needed this so badly! This past week of writing has had its ups and downs. A day away would do me some good and give me a chance to recuperate.

As we made our way up the I-17, Joe and I began talking about the book. He made a comment that sent me spiraling back into the tears and heartache once again. I had been doing remarkably well, with no crying the past five days. This shit really tears you open and exposes the rawness of it all. He hit a nerve, and I couldn't stop it from happening. I've heard from several people over the past few weeks that, what I'm going through is a form of PTSD. Maybe it is. I won't use it as a crutch. I have too much life left to live and way too much to look forward to. I'm certainly not going to mock it either, because it should be taken seriously, no matter what. Writing is how I deal with things. I don't take any drugs what so ever. I do take vitamins in order to keep me healthy. I don't smoke anything. I have maybe one or two drinks max a week. Enough said about that.

The comment he made had something to do with my daughter and losing her. He apparently didn't remember all the details, and he thought I had let her go of my own free will in order to save her. NOT HARDLY! It wasn't my choice! I wish I had been stronger at the time. I am stronger now, which helps me in telling this story. He then went on to say something to the effect of, how could a normal person read this book, or even want to. Through my tears, I told him that this isn't about a normal person reading this book. This is not only for me to heal and to clear the air, so that my children can better understand it, but it's also for others. People who have lived it. People who are around people who have lived it, and they don't quite understand it. People who are living it now and don't know how to have a voice to end the cycle.

What defines normal? To be honest, I don't believe that anyone is normal in this world. We have all had shit happen to us in one way or another. It's how we deal with it that defines our character and who we become. Some choose to play the victim, because it gets them attention. I would prefer to be on the strong side and live my life the best way I can. I'm no angel. I've done things in my life, and I'm certainly far from perfect. I wouldn't want to be perfect. It's my flaws and my mistakes that help me to learn and grow as a person.

This story is not for everyone, and some will find it hard to stomach. I hope it reaches out and speaks to many. If you are a father to a young girl, please make sure to be there for her, and let her know what's right from what's wrong. Be the kind of man who will protect her and not tell her, "No, don't do that." If you tell her not to see a boy, she's not going to listen to you. You have to approach it from a real standpoint. Always be honest with her. Let her know it's her heart that's most important, and you will be there for her if she needs you. If my father would have been there for me emotionally, and been the kind of dad he should have been, Mike would never have been allowed to mess with me, or live in our family home.

Mothers, if you have a daughter, please let her know you are available for her as well. Never be afraid to educate your daughter and get down and dirty about the facts of life. Let her know the lines of communication are open. Don't ignore the signs. This also goes for parents who have a son. Please make sure you raise a well-adjusted man and not someone who emotionally or physically abuses people. Don't be afraid to be open and honest with your children. You will have a much better relationship with them, and they will make you proud as an adult. If you are a parent who has a tough time with your children, and you strike out emotionally or physically, STOP IT! Get the help you need before your child becomes a messed-up adult. Break the damn cycle! Remember, you're raising a future adult.

This is the 21st century, and it really pisses me off to see that this still exists even more so in this world today. We can't change the whole world, but we can start with one person at a time. It scares the hell out of me that I have a very well-adjusted son raising his own two children right now, and who knows what kind of people they will encounter when they grow up? You can bet as long as I'm around, I will not allow anyone to harm my grandchildren. They will come to understand what is right and wrong in other's behavior. They will never be afraid to come to me or their parents with anything. I wish I had someone like that in my life during my younger years. It may have saved me from the hell I lived through. Let's get back to the story, shall we?

I should have been questioning Mike about the whole Debbie mess, but I didn't. That issue seemed to just disappear, and it was never brought up again. I was so caught up in planning the wedding and taking care of my son. I didn't have time to think about it. Why shouldn't I believe him, right? He came back to us and wanted to be with me and his child.

The day of the wedding came and went without a hitch, so I thought. I found out later that day, a few things were slightly off kilter. The grassy area where we had planned to have the ceremony was a mess, because they had irrigated the park. The guys had to move all the chairs onto the concrete area. The fountain was supposed to be going, but it was down for repairs. The park was littered with dead birds, and the guys made sure to remove all of them before any of the guests or I arrived. If the bird thing wasn't bad enough, we ended up putting his wedding ring on the wrong hand during the ceremony. Do you think the universe was trying to tell me something that day? Too bad I didn't listen to the message.

Now that we were married, it was time for us to get our own place. I'm not sure why Mike didn't want to look for a house. He chose a mobile home instead. We moved into a park down off of

Arizona Avenue and Ray Rd. called Chandler Meadows. Not exactly the life I had envisioned for myself, but it was our own place.

Things seemed to be going along fine at first, but he wasn't too thrilled with me wanting to do more in the radio and entertainment industry. I had to quit working in radio and not have much contact with friends. I remember working on Bill and Ted's Excellent Adventure for three nights in a row. Seven o'clock p.m. to seven a.m. was the set time. I had bought him a little finch, since we couldn't have a dog. I asked him to cover the bird every night while I went to work on the set. Every morning I came home, I found the bird hadn't been covered. On the last day, I came home and found a dead bird. I'm not sure if he did anything to it other than not cover it at night. I was heartbroken.

That's not even the worst thing. Jeffrey had developed a very bad rash, because Mike had gotten lazy and didn't bother changing his diaper as often as he should have. It was piss and poop soaked every morning. Unbelievable! And you call yourself a parent. My ass! I asked why he didn't change him and put Desitin on the rash. No answer, just a glare from him as he walked away.

Things began to fall back into the same pattern of the old days. He would belittle me from time to time. He would tell me what I could and couldn't wear. I basically left my career in the dust, because he didn't want me to have any kind of life outside of our home. Day after day he had a routine he would follow. He would come home from work, have me go in the bedroom, get undressed, and he would do his thing. Once he finished, he would go into the living room, get himself a soda, light a cigarette and chill out on the recliner in front of the television. He just left me on the bed like I was nothing. I felt like nothing. I wanted to die. I was so numb. It wouldn't happen every day, and I was thankful for that.

It wasn't long after this that I found out I was pregnant again. I had started spotting one day and didn't really think anything of it at first. I was still taking birth control, so why would I be worried? After a few days, I started to get a really bad side ache. I told Mike about it, and he suggested I go to the doctor and find out what was going on. They did a piss test and it came back positive for being pregnant. Talk about freaking me out! I was on birth control both times and ended up pregnant both times! What gives?

I didn't know how Mike was going to take the news. I had a talk with him when he got home that night. My memory is foggy as to the actual words that were spoken. All I can remember is him saying not to tell anyone about the baby right now. I didn't know why he would say something like that. Why wasn't he excited? I was scared at the time, and again, I let him control the situation. I didn't really have a choice.

CHAPTER NINE

No one should ever be bullied into making a decision, especially one concerning a child. In my life back then, it was a daily occurrence. I was afraid of my own shadow, because I never knew what was going to set him off. I was young, naive and scared to death of the man who claimed he loved me. Love should never be a word thrown around lightly or used to control someone.

You would have thought this man would be happy to have a son, and another child on the way, with the woman he just married and claimed to be in love with. I questioned it all the time, since I was living this daily nightmare that never seemed to end. How could he do this to me? How could he do this to us? How could he do this to his son? Why on earth did he marry me? I couldn't understand all of this at the time. I have a much clearer picture now. It was about control. It was always about control.

Over the next several months, things continued as they always did. Sex in the bedroom at his command. Being left on the bed alone as he smoked his cigarette and drank his soda in front of the television. Not being able to tell anyone the hell I was living, because of the daily threats. "Keep quiet and don't tell anyone, or I will kill you," as he pointed to the gun rack on the wall that held his two 22 rifles. He wanted no one to know about me being pregnant. I felt helpless and hopeless. The only thing that kept me going was my son Jeffrey. He needed me, and I was the only one he could rely on.

I can remember a night when our friends Debi and Jerry came over to play cards. There was a movie on the television in the background. A woman was testifying on the stand during a trial. The prosecutor asked her several questions that froze me. "Was your husband raping you? Did you want to have sex with him, or did he force you? Was it against your will?" As I heard these words, a tear began to fall down my cheek. Debi apparently saw this, and she made a comment out loud as she looked at Mike. "Are you raping your wife?" He laughed and told her, "Of course not. She just gets really emotional when she watches those kinds of movies." What I thought was a potential lifeline for me, disappeared in the blink of an eye. I was alone in my hell once again.

Things began to escalate in the worst of ways. I needed to tell my family about the baby. I still wasn't showing yet, and he continued to tell me I needed to keep quiet. When I brought up the fact I would be showing by my eighth month, like I did with Jeffrey, he raised his voice and said, "If you say anything to anyone, I will kill Jeffrey, make you watch, then I will kill you." Yes, it was getting quite ugly.

Anytime someone mentioned I was gaining weight, he would tell them I was taking a new medication which caused that to happen. I still can't fathom today how anyone believed the shit that would come out of his mouth. Then again, I believed him when he said those vows to me. To love, honor and cherish me 'till death do us part. Maybe that was his intention. Maybe he wanted to kill me. I had no idea. I just lived in fear, and that's how he controlled me.

As the daily rituals continued, I found myself growing more and more depressed. How was I going to be a good mother to both of my children, living in an environment like this? Why was he doing this? Didn't he understand right from wrong? Why did I have to live in fear like this? I was consumed with it all. I was terrified he would kill me in my sleep, or worse, hurt or kill Jeffrey. I couldn't handle that. I couldn't lose my son at the hands of his father. I had to do something.

My mom had been giving me copies of her magazine *True Story*. I would read these as an escape from my daily hell. One day, I read a story about a woman who had used something called Spanish fly to poison her husband and kill him. Her situation was different than mine. Her husband cheated on her, and she killed him out of revenge.

I didn't even know if Mike was faithful to me. I couldn't even concern myself with that during this time. All I could think about was surviving every day and doing my best to protect my children at any cost. I wasn't sure I was physically capable of doing that. All I knew is that I had to find a way.

I noticed an advertisement in the back of the magazine for sexual enhancement items. One of them happened to be Spanish fly. It was only a few bucks for a small bottle. I stared at that page for what seemed like forever. I closed the magazine. I had to forget the thoughts that were running through my mind. I found myself opening the magazine to that page several times over the next few days. I cried. It was tormenting. How could I even be thinking of doing this? I just couldn't. I'm not a killer! I closed the magazine again and left it closed for the time being.

It wasn't long now until the baby would be born. On the next visit to the obstetrician, we found out we were going to have a girl. I was excited, because now I would have one of each: a boy and a girl. I already had a name picked out: Ashley Yvonne. Mike didn't seem excited at all, and I couldn't understand why. Now we had some real news to share about the baby, and I thought he might be ready to tell the family. I brought it up again, and I was shut down with the same threats I was used to hearing. I just couldn't grasp what was happening.

He came home from work one day and wanted to talk about the baby. This was unusual. I was happy. I was thinking we were going to tell the family. That was so not the case. He said we should consider some options. What the hell was he talking about? Options? He said we should put the baby up for adoption, because we couldn't afford it. Adoption? Why would he even suggest this? I don't remember the rest of the conversation. My mind has blocked it out.

My heart was aching, and I felt as if I had just dropped into a black hole. How can this really be love if this man wants to discard his own flesh and blood so easily? I felt so numb. I didn't know what to do. Who could I go to that would believe me? Could I even risk telling anyone and not have something happen to Jeffrey or myself? I lived with this day after day. I cried and cried. I screamed out for someone to help me. I was so lost.

I was cleaning the kitchen one day, trying to get my mind off of things. I ran across the magazine. I found myself looking at that page again. I'm not sure how long I was staring at it. You know when you become fixated on an object, and you lose all track of time? That was me in this moment. Tears were streaming down my cheeks, as the words were playing over and over in my head. "Don't tell anyone or I will kill Jeff, make you watch, and then I will kill you. We need to consider some options. Adoption. We can't afford this kid." This was my hell!

I couldn't take it anymore. I picked up the phone, called the number on the ad and ordered a bottle of Spanish fly. I wasn't really thinking clearly. I closed the magazine and put it away, never looking at it again. A week went by, and the same old routine continued in my home. I was in survival mode and pretty much did whatever he told me to do. I couldn't risk him hurting any of us.

The weekend was right around the corner. Weekends were always the toughest here at home. It meant I would have to deal with him being around 24-7. At least on the weekdays, I had a bit of a reprieve with him working all day. This Friday was a little bit different for me. When I went to the mailbox, I found a small package along with the regular mail. Once I got back into the house, I opened up the package. I was a bit surprised by the contents. It was the bottle of Spanish fly. I had completely forgotten I had ordered it. I found myself staring at it and again hearing his words in my head over and over. "Don't tell anyone, or I will kill Jeff, make you watch, and then I will kill you. We need to consider some options. Adoption. We can't afford this kid."

I hated my fucking life! What should have been one of the happiest times in my life, was turning out to be very torturous. My mom should have been able to celebrate the coming birth of her granddaughter. She should have been able to be there for me, helping to decorate the nursery as she did before her grandson was born. Both of us were being cheated out of this. The only thing that gave me any peace, was being able to have my son with me, and to also speak to my baby girl while she lay inside my womb.

I kept staring at that bottle, and I could still hear those words in my head. I finally shook it off and came back to reality. I took the bottle and hid it in the kitchen drawer beneath the towels. I would throw it away after the weekend was over, and he wouldn't see it in the trash. I didn't need him to see that bottle. God only knows what he would have done to me.

He came home from work not long after that. He had one thing on his mind, as usual. You would think, since I was pregnant and had a big belly, that it would be a deterrent for him. Not the case. So the same shit happened that always did. His demands were met, and he left me back in that room, all alone once again. Something happened that was a little bit different that afternoon. As he got up to leave the room, he said he was going to take a shower. He wanted me to get up and get him a glass of soda, so he would have it when he got out of the shower. He had never asked me to do that before.

I grabbed my clothes, got dressed and went into the kitchen. I felt so numb, like I always did. I could feel the tears running down my face. Is this what marriage is supposed to be? I didn't really know. It's not the kind of life I had envisioned for myself or my children. So much for the fairy tales I used to read when I was a little girl. This life was certainly no fairy tale for me. It was more like a daily nightmare I could never wake up from.

I was thankful Jeffrey was still asleep in his playpen. He didn't need to see his mommy like this. I was a mess. I wiped the tears from my face and went about getting his glass of soda ready. I put several ice cubes in and began to pour the soda. I stopped midway through and started crying again, as I noticed Jeffrey was stirring in the playpen. I'm not sure how long I was staring at him, but I knew I had to get the glass of soda ready before Mike got out there. I didn't want to give him any ammunition to start in on me.

I again wiped the tears from my face and finished pouring the soda. I overfilled the glass and spilled some on the counter top. I was looking for a towel, but couldn't find one. I had to get the mess cleaned up. I opened up the drawer to get a towel. There it was, staring me right in the face. That bottle of Spanish fly. I started tearing up again. I found myself reaching into the drawer to get a towel, but instead grabbed the bottle. I stared at it in my hand for a few minutes. I kept hearing his words in my head as the tears came down my face. "Don't tell anyone. I will kill Jeffrey, make you watch, then kill you. Keep quiet about the baby. Don't tell anyone. We need to consider some options. Adoption. We can't afford this kid."

Those words were pounding over and over in my head. I wanted to scream, but couldn't. I didn't want to wake Jeffrey. I just started crying and shaking. I found myself opening the bottle, and I poured the entire thing into the glass of soda. I just stared at the glass, watching the condensation on the side and listening to the fizz of the carbonation. Could I really do this? Could I really kill him? I would be free of his bullshit, his threats and his control. I wouldn't lose my baby. The kids and I could be free of his wrath once and for all.

Just then, I was startled by the sound of his voice. "You got my soda ready?" I saw him coming down the hallway and his voice woke Jeffrey up. I grabbed the glass of soda off the counter and dumped it into the sink, completely emptying it. "What the fuck did you do that for," he said. I made up some excuse that I had seen a fly in his drink, so I chose to empty it and give him a clean glass. He just replied for me to hurry up and get it to him.

I couldn't do it. Why couldn't I do it? Why couldn't I end this damn nightmare I had been living? I had a conscience. I knew I would be doing something wrong, no matter how I tried to justify my reasons for doing it. No person is worth going to jail over. I would have definitely lost my life, and it would have cost me my children in the worst of ways if I had killed him that day. I could have done the world a big favor by taking him off this earth. He wouldn't have been able to abuse others down the road as he did. As someone had told me recently, I was just practice.

CHAPTER TEN

Things continued on as they always did. I struggled with the idea that I had come close to killing him. I had a nightmare one night where I went through with it, but he took one sip and knew the soda had been poisoned. He threw the glass at me, hitting me in the head. That sent me flying to the floor. He screamed at me, "You fucking bitch! How dare you try to kill me! It's time for me to teach you a lesson!" He went over to the wall, grabbed one of the 22 rifles from the rack, cocked it and shot Jeffrey. I could hear myself screaming as he turned the gun on me. I woke up as the blast went off. How much more of this shit was I going to have to deal with? It's not bad enough I go through this all the time while I'm awake, and now my dreams were being invaded by him! My dreams were always an escape, but now I needed to escape from them.

The best thing I had to look forward to was Jeffrey's upcoming first birthday party. Mike said we should do it at my mom's house, because he didn't want to have our house full of people. I didn't question it at the time, but I think I knew why he didn't want anyone there. When we were at home, his behavior was so different. At other's homes, or out in public, he was so charming and was able to fool everyone for the most part. I noticed a weird trend with him over the years. Any time we took pictures together, or someone took his, he never smiled. He always looked angry. I wish I had paid closer attention at the time. I may have seen the real him before it was too late.

Jeffrey's birthday was finally here. I was a bit uncomfortable when several people mentioned my weight gain. Again, Mike told them it was a side effect of the medication I was taking. What medication was I supposed to be taking? No one ever asked, and he never said. He would just glare at me, and I knew I couldn't say anything. So much for being able to tell anyone who could rescue me from my daily hell.

Sometime during the party, I felt a little strange. I went to the bathroom and realized that I was going into labor. I had to let Mike know without alerting anyone else there. He told everyone he needed to take me to the hospital, because I was having a bad reaction to my new medication. I look back on that time now and wonder how anyone could even think this was true. It just goes to show you how easy it was for him to charm and lie to others.

We made our way to the hospital, and within a short amount of time, my baby girl was born by C-section. I don't remember much about this time. Apparently I had some scar tissue from my previous C-section, and they decided to clean it up a bit. I do remember seeing my baby and holding her a few times. I even fed her twice. I remember one morning when I awoke, I went down to the nursery to see her. The nurse told me that the people had already come and taken her. I didn't know what she meant, so I asked if it were my husband or my parents who had taken her. She replied, "No, the people from the adoption agency."

I have no recall of what came next. I was told by the nurse that I was very upset and crying hysterically. I had apparently trashed a nurse's station and part of the lobby. Sometimes I wish I could remember. Other times, I'm glad I can't. It's hard enough as it is to know I lost my child that day.

I had the perfect situation. Two kids, a boy and a girl, born on the same day, one year apart. How often does something like this happen? I would have the best birthdays every year, because both kids would be able to celebrate with each other on the same day. No arguments, because one kid got presents and the other one didn't. No fighting over it, and no crying. Just perfect harmony. That wasn't meant to be for me. My heart had been ripped out along with my baby.

I had no recall of signing the adoption papers, or when it even took place, until about 12 years ago. I underwent hypnosis for past life regression in a class that I was taking at a local bookstore. Once we all came out of it, we were asked to share what we had remembered. I had several things come out of it, but one thing in particular really blew my mind. I saw myself, Mike and a woman, who was obviously the adoption caseworker, sitting in a van parked in front of the lumber company. I saw myself crying as the caseworker put the paperwork in front of me to read. She asked me if I was sure I wanted to do this. I didn't have a choice in the matter. He glared at me and made sure I agreed to do it.

Maybe deep down inside I knew this was for the best, because she could get away from this bastard and have a chance at a normal life. I don't know what I was thinking at the time. I just did what I was told. I've included a scan of the actual adoption agreement in the back of the book. Where is my signature? It's not there. It's only signed by him. My signature should have been required for this to have happened!

For the next several months, my life was a blur. I just went through the motions day by day. An incident that comes to mind, really set things in motion for this relationship to come to an end. I'm not sure how long it was after the baby had been born, but I had another pregnancy scare. I felt a weirdness in my body that seemed all too familiar. I assumed I was pregnant again. How could this be? I was under a doctor's care for birth control and I'm going through this shit yet again?

I brought my fears up to Mike, and his comment to me was, "If you are pregnant again, we'll just keep this one and raise it as a challenge." Excuse me? Did I hear you correctly? "If you are pregnant again, we'll just keep this one and raise it as a challenge?" Those words echoed in my head over and over. I couldn't believe he would say something like that to me. I knew there was no way in hell I wanted another child by this man, after what he had put me through, and the way I had lost my daughter. I didn't want her to come back in my life down the road and see I had a child after her. She wouldn't understand why she was given up and how we could have had another child after her, who we did keep. That would destroy her.

I went to the doctor and they ran a test. It turned out to be negative, THANK GOD! I went home and shared the news with Mike. He didn't seem to care either way. Things just went on as they always did. I came to the conclusion that my life would continue down this path if I didn't do something to change it. I called the doctor and asked about options for a more permanent solution. They wanted to see me in the office to discuss this, because as they put it, "I was way too young to be thinking about such a thing."

I didn't want to bring this up to Mike until I got a chance to discuss things with the doctor. This was MY choice, and for once I would have MY choice, no matter what. Hell yes, I was scared of everything, but I certainly did not want another child with this man. I couldn't go through that kind of hell again. I went to meet with the doctor a few days later to see what options I had. They mentioned a procedure called a tubal ligation, where they cut and burn the ends of the tubes. It had a pretty good success rate, and very few women ever regrew their tubes back. It sounded like the right thing for me to do. I wasn't sure about how to bring this up to Mike. I didn't know how he would take this idea. I was worried he wouldn't let me do it. He had to sign off on it if I were to have the surgery. I was worried if I brought it up, it would send him over the edge, and he would do something to hurt Jeffrey and me.

CHAPTER ELEVEN

It's not an easy thing going over the past events and sharing all of the details in this book. As a survivor, we all know you must be able to get past the events in order to heal the wounds that have been left behind. They will never completely heal, but getting your story out there sure does help in the process. I have to unlock the secrets of my past and share them on a grand scale with the world. Many of you, who have known me personally, do have some insight into the events I have gone through. Others know only parts of the story. I'm not one to cause or create drama. I will never play victim or try to gain sympathy from others. I am just a survivor trying to live my life as best as I can.

What started me on this whole journey back in late July, was a message that my son had received from Mike. Jeff was trying to be a big brother and protect his sister. He was worried she was falling prey to Mike's manipulations, so he friended his biological father on Facebook. I had no idea he had done this. When I found out, you can imagine how upset I was to see this.

Jeffrey basically wanted to play nice with Mike to get at the truth and to see what he had been saying to his sister. My son is a good man, but he went about things the wrong way. His sister has never had a chance to bond with us. She has never even met us. We have tried on several occasions to get her out here to meet everyone, but it never worked out. I guess she wasn't ready, and I wasn't going to push either. She is an adult and has to make up her own mind about things. I never told her everything about the ugliness that took place. I didn't think it was necessary at the time when I first spoke with her almost 10 years ago.

My son wrote to Mike saying he wanted to hear his side of the story. He told Jeff he may not like what he hears, but he would tell him the truth. I could only wish he had told the truth. I was hoping the letter in return would take responsibility for his actions and say we both did things. I hoped he would have apologized for what he had done and asked for forgiveness. Not the case at all.

His letter had about 10% truth and 90% bullshit in it. He told partial truths on a couple of things, but managed to leave out the important details. He also combined details of his marriage to me and his second marriage. He meshed his second wife and me together as one person. What is wrong with his memory that he can't distinguish between the details of his two different wives from two different marriages?

This letter really upset me. If he was telling this kind of shit to my son, who knows most of it is a lie, then what the hell has he said to my daughter? I'm sure you're asking right now, why on earth would she even talk to the man who wanted nothing to do with her and who ripped her away from her family when she was a baby? Good question. As I said, she is an adult and has to make up her own mind. Unfortunately, he is a master manipulator, and one could only hope she is strong enough to not get sucked into his bullshit. That letter was my motivation to set the record straight, no matter how ugly or painful it was.

I warned you in the beginning that it can get pretty gritty at times. I won't make up shit to cover the gaps in my memory. I will just let the details pour out of the recesses of my brain. I won't sugarcoat it either. You're going to get the raw data, and you can do with it what you will. For me, the journey into the past continues on, and once we reach that point, I will reveal Mike's letter to my son word-for-word. Then I will break it down sentence-by-sentence and share the correct details to clear up any of the bullshit. The truth is on my side. Now back to my story.

I knew I had to get that surgery done. What choice did I have at this point? I didn't want to continue living with the thought that I could get pregnant yet again by this man. My heart couldn't take it. I decided I would bring it up during dinner that night. I was being brave, but it didn't work out in my favor, as it never did. He was silent at first, and then he got upset with me. He didn't want to hear about me "getting fixed." That was the end of it, for now.

So much of my life was a blur after I lost my baby girl. I grew despondent and mainly just tried to survive living on a daily basis. My son is what kept me going. I can't recall most of the days back then. I only remember bits and pieces. As I said before, I will never make up details to fill in the spaces. I can only speak the truth as to what I remember going through. I have flashbacks once in a while. I see the same things going on. The sexual abuse, the emotional torment, the threats of taking my life. He didn't even realize he had already taken my life in so many other ways than actually killing me. Sometimes I wished I was already dead, but then I would think about my son, and realize death was not an option for me.

There was one weekend that could have ended my life, and he had nothing to do with it. We had gone over to pick up Jeffrey from his visit with his grandparents. They asked us to stay for dinner, and we left just after dark. We were stopped at the light at Arizona Avenue and Ray Rd., just around the corner from our house. Out of nowhere, a vehicle slammed into the car, and I felt the full force of the impact. The car sped off. Thank God several people witnessed the crash and called the police. I remember being scared and looking back at Jeffrey. He appeared fine, since he was sitting in his car seat behind Mike and not me. If he had been behind me, he might not be here today.

A man had followed the other driver from the freeway and managed to get the license plate on the car. He said the driver appeared drunk and was weaving all over the road. He said he had paced the car a few times, and was going in excess of 70 mph most of the time. If they hadn't followed him, we would have never known who hit us. We were checked out by emergency personnel, and we all seemed fine. They said to follow up with our doctor if we needed to. The cops tracked down the car later that night. They arrested the young man who had caused the accident and left the scene.

The next morning, I awoke in major pain. I called my parents to let them know what had happened, and they suggested I go see their chiropractor. I got an emergency appointment and went to see him. They did x-rays and it turned out that the vertebrae in both my neck and lower back had completely twisted itself. There was also a slight tear in my neck, thanks to the jolt I had when the car was hit. The chiropractor told me, if the tear had been just a 16th of an inch more, I most likely would have been paralyzed from the neck down. Not something I wanted to hear. I went through intense treatments for the next five months and then moderate treatments for the next three months: over eight months to get through this and still trying to deal with everything else.

During this time, the insurance company wanted to go after the other driver, so they pursued legal action. Apparently he was underage, drunk and driving his mother's car. The insurance was due to expire the day after the accident. I'm glad it happened when it did, or I would have been on the hook for all of the medical bills. I don't remember what the settlement was. I know it basically covered all of the medical bills, which I was happy about. In fact, I have no recollection of us getting any money outside of the medical being paid off.

It wasn't long after this that I had gone back to work. I took a job managing a phone room. It wasn't really my thing, but it helped to pay the bills. I remember we had bought my dad's car, a 1971 Chrysler Newport Royal. The damn thing was a huge four-door boat I hated driving, but I had no choice at the time. It was payday, and I had the day off. Mike wanted me to go get my paycheck. He also made a demand that day, because he knew I liked talking to my co-workers. "Don't shut the car off, and don't take Jeff out. Get your check, and get back home." I so wish I hadn't listened to him.

I drove down to work to get my paycheck. His words kept echoing in my head. "Don't shut the car off, and don't take Jeff out. Get your check, and get back home." So I did as I was told. I pulled up out front of my office and left the car running, with Jeff strapped in his car seat in the back passenger side. My office was located in the middle of a strip mall on the southeast corner of Stapley and Broadway. I was inside less than a minute, but that was all it took. I came back out and saw the car moving across the parking lot. I ran after it as fast as I could!

I caught up to it and tried to grab the door to open it. I got thrown under the front tire and the car ran over me. The car crashed into the front of a little craft store that was on the end of the strip mall. I was freaked! I got up from the ground and limped my way over to the car. Jeff was sitting in the front seat laughing. I was so thankful that he appeared to be okay. The paramedics showed up a few minutes later, and they checked him over. They also noticed I was cut up and bleeding in several places. I didn't realize I had gotten hurt. I was too worried about my little boy.

The car didn't have much damage, thanks to being built like a tank. It's probably the reason why Jeff didn't get hurt either. You would think that Mike would have felt a little guilty about what happened. Nope. All he cared about was the slight front-end damage on the car and the possibility of getting sued by the owner of the craft store. He wasn't even the least bit concerned about Jeff or me. I felt extremely guilty that I had let him bully me into doing something that could have turned out a lot worse. The insurance company settled with the store owner and repaired the damage to the front wall. No lawsuit at all against us. That was a good thing. I have no idea what he would have done to me if that had happened.

I don't remember much about the following months. I spent my days just existing. I had an overwhelming ache deep down inside for my baby girl, and the depression grew worse. Living in a blind haze, I continued to do as I was told. I barely had the energy or strength to even try to fight it. I thank God for my son, or I wouldn't have survived this existence.

Things began to spiral out of control in late 1987. I can't recall what the argument was about, but he really got in my face this time. He shoved me, and I went flying back into the bar counter top. As I stumbled to get back on my feet, my face felt really hot, and my right ear began to sting. I took my hand, put it up to my ear and felt something wet and sharp. I looked at my hand and noticed it was now red. This was my blood! That son of a bitch drew my blood! I had fallen against the scissor blade that was on the counter top, and it went into the back of my ear. Something in me just snapped, and I finally woke up from my daze. That was the turning point in our relationship.

I removed the scissors and threw them down on the floor. I grabbed a towel and placed it up to my ear to wipe away the blood. I wasn't bleeding too badly, but it was enough to piss me off. I went over to him, and by this time, he was sitting in the recliner. I grabbed him by the back of the hairline and pulled him up off of the chair. I dragged him over to the wall where those rifles were. I slammed his head up against that wall at least a half a dozen times. I can still hear those words in my head today. "How does it feel you son of a bitch? How do you fucking like it? How does is it feel, mother fucker?"

I was so angry. I could have probably killed him right then and there. I exhausted myself and finally let him go. He fell down to the floor. He wasn't too happy with me. He got up from the floor, looked at me with contempt and stormed out of the room. No words were spoken. I expected him to beat the hell out of me, but he didn't touch me. I'm sure he realized, I wasn't the same anymore, and I would no longer put up with his bullshit. It was the first time I had felt free in a long time.

CHAPTER TWELVE

Not much was said during the days that followed. He came and went in silence. For the first time in our relationship, I felt like I was gaining control over my own life. I felt like I could finally breathe. As we approached the next weekend, he broke his silence with a vengeance. He started off with his demands, but this time, he got an argument from me. I wasn't about to back down now when I felt as if I had gotten free of his controlling wrath. "You're my wife, and you will do what I say," he said. My response surprised even me. "I'm your wife, not your fucking slave! I don't have to do shit for you, if I don't want to!"

He seemed a bit shocked that I had spoken to him like that. He was so used to getting his way, and he realized in that moment, his grip on me was loosening up day by day. I expected him to strike me, but he didn't. He just told me to fuck off and sat in his recliner. I wasn't quite finished showing off my new empowerment, so I went for the bonus of telling him to go fuck himself. Well, he wasn't going to have that be the last word. He started yelling at me, calling me all kinds of names.

Our argument was interrupted by a phone call from his grandmother. He said something in the background that made her respond very negatively towards me. My words to her are so very clear to this day. "I'm not the bad person here," I said starting to cry. It all came flooding out, and I was so relieved to finally be able to tell the truth without fearing the worst. "Do you know what your damn grandson did to me? He took my baby and put her up for adoption! I lost my child because of him! He's been threatening me and Jeffrey for a long time now."

I'm sure I stunned her with this revelation. I can't even remember her response to what I had said. I just remember seeing him get up from the recliner, shoot me a dirty look and storm off. He went into the bedroom and slammed the door, locking it behind him. I'm not sure if she hung up on me or if I hung up the phone. I don't remember much about the rest of that night, other than sleeping on the couch.

The following morning, I made my way back to the bedroom so I could shower and get dressed. The door was locked. He was still in there and was refusing to come out. I kept knocking on the door, asking him to open it up so I could get my clothes. All I heard was, "Leave me the fuck alone!" So with that, I went back into the living room to wait him out. Several hours went by, and I decided to try it again. This time he was just silent.

I went back into the living room and made a phone call to my folks. We were supposed to pick up Jeffrey from his weekend visit with them and stay for dinner. I had to let them know we weren't going to make it over, since he had locked himself in the bedroom and was refusing to come out. I would have left to get Jeffrey myself, but Mike had the car keys. I don't recall what else was said during the conversation with my folks. I do remember, a short time later, several people showing up at the house. I'm not sure who all came over, but I know one of them was my Uncle John.

The memory of him being there is so vivid. You could say, my uncle was a larger than life character, with a booming voice and attitude that would scare the hell out of most people. He could be quite boisterous at times. I wouldn't want him to be any other way. His voice echoed through the house as he shouted a few obscenities towards Mike. "What a pussy, locking yourself in the bedroom and pouting. Knock that shit off! C'mon you big pussy, get out here and act like a real man. Stop acting like a fucking baby." It makes me laugh now when I think about it. Back then, I was quite scared he would come out of that room and attack my uncle, or go after me. But then again, attacking women was more his style. My uncle would have pounded his ass into the ground either way. I would have loved to see that.

Things quieted down after a while as we sat down and were talking. I can't remember the conversation, or who I was talking to. A little while later, Mike made his way out of the bedroom, and we could tell he wasn't too happy by the scowl on his face. He went past everyone into to the kitchen, got out a soda and sat on his recliner. Nothing was said. He just looked at me as if he wanted to kill me. Everyone left, and the house was silent for the rest of the day.

When it came time to go pick up Jeffrey, I mentioned it to him, and he didn't say anything. He just grabbed the keys and made his way out the door. The silence in the car was hard to take. I felt like I was finally finding my voice, but yet I was forced to remain silent, for fear of upsetting him and causing more problems. We arrived at my parent's house with no issues. Mom was in the kitchen making dinner, so I asked if she needed any help. Mike went into the living room and watched television, not saying much of anything to anyone.

After dinner, we were playing cards, and he began to argue with me. He was demanding I put the title of my car in his name. Not both of our names, just HIS name. My car was an older Opel Manta he had tried to turn into a Knight Rider Kitt car. I stood up to him and said I wouldn't do that, especially after what he did with my first car back when we were dating. He got very angry with me and started saying nasty things to me. That's when the shit really hit the fan.

My mom stood up and slammed her fist on the table. "She is not going to put the title in your name! That's her car her grandparents left her money to buy. That is not your car!" I had never seen my mom do that before. I was stunned to say the least! The mama bear in her finally came out to protect her baby.

Mike was very surprised by her reaction, and he didn't like it at all. He got up from the table and threw down his cards. He then walked over to the front door. I got up from the table and looked in his direction. I had no idea what was about to happen, and I certainly didn't expect what came next. He removed his wedding ring and threw it on the floor. He then threw the keys at me and said, "You can take your daughter and her car and shove them up your ass where the sun don't shine!" He walked out the door and slammed it behind him.

We were all a bit stunned at what had just happened. I sat down with my folks and revealed the details of what brought everything on. My mom was devastated to hear about the baby. She said that she had a feeling I was pregnant back when Mike was telling everyone I was gaining weight due to the medication. It was such a relief to finally have all of it out in the open. I felt a huge weight lifted off of my shoulders. This was a day I would never forget, December 12, 1987.

I waited at their house until almost 9:00 p.m., and still no sign of Mike. I wasn't sure if he had walked home or went somewhere else. It was getting late, so I had to pack up Jeffrey's stuff and get him home. Mom asked me if I wanted to stay there for the night, but I said I needed to go home. I didn't know what to expect when I arrived home. Would he be there? Would he hurt Jeffrey or me? What was to come of us and this hell of a marriage? I should have been happy he walked out that door, but I was scared and feeling so alone.

I went by the front of the house and didn't see him sitting on the steps. I parked in the driveway, and there was no sign of him at all outside. He wouldn't be able to get inside unless he broke in. I unlocked the door and went in. The house was silent. Nothing had been disturbed. He had not come home at all. Where could he be? I had a hard time sleeping that night, because I didn't know if he would show up and do anything to us in the middle of the night. I was expecting the worst.

Things were a bit awkward the next morning. I was so used to him dictating to me what my day was going to be like. Not today. He was nowhere around. In fact, he didn't come home or call for several days. I should have been dancing with happiness, but it wasn't like that at all. I was heartbroken. I felt abandoned. What was I going to do without him? What would Jeffrey do without his daddy around? I was so confused.

What the hell was wrong with me to be feeling like that? Why should I even give a damn about this man who treated me like shit all these years and cost me my child? I didn't understand it all back then, but I do now. It's what abused people go through. You are so used to being beaten down all the time, that you feel lost when the abuser is no longer around. It takes time to get over this and become healthy again. I didn't know it at the time, but this whole experience would be responsible for who I am today. I am strong, I don't take any shit, and most important, I value myself.

Over the next few days, I made several phone calls to friends and other family members to see if they knew where he was. Apparently he had moved in with our friends Jerry and Debi. God only knows what he had told them. These were the same two people who would come over to our house and play cards with us. She was also the one who had asked if he had been raping his wife.

They must have heard I was looking for him, because Debi called me. Mike had her do it. He couldn't even be bothered to call me himself. She said he wanted to come and get his stuff from the house. At this point, I didn't want him inside the house with us. I had no idea what would happen if we were alone with him. I told her he could come by over the weekend. I said I would bag up all of his clothes and make sure all of his belongings would be out on the porch for him. The strong side of me was very apparent that day.

I spent the next two days going through everything in the house to make sure I packed all of his stuff. I didn't want to be accused of taking anything that belonged to him. I found myself struggling with all of this. One minute, I felt relieved I would no longer have to be treated like dirt on a daily basis. The next, I would break down and cry. Back then, I thought I was losing someone I loved. I didn't really know what love was. Today I know better.

Once Saturday arrived, I moved everything out on the porch and locked up the house. There was no way I was going to let him back inside. Sometime that day, he came by and picked everything up. I didn't have to deal with him at all. I'm sure he would have tried to start something if there weren't others there with him. It was just his style. Now I had to deal with what was to come next...the unknown. I should have been celebrating his departure from my life, but it wasn't that simple. As we all know, when you are married and it ends, you still have to deal with the other person, especially if you have children with them.

I was also struggling with Christmas being right around the corner. I made a decision to not put up a tree at the house. In all honesty, I couldn't afford it, but the thought of it made me sick to my stomach. Even the sound of Christmas carols made me ill. How could I celebrate this holiday, when my husband walked out on me and left me to care for our young two year old by myself? I decided to pack a few things so Jeffrey and I could stay with my folks. I didn't feel it was right to make my son miss out on stuff, just because I felt like crap.

The holiday came and went. No sign of Mike. Not even a phone call. You would have thought he'd want to see his son for Christmas, or bring him presents. Nothing at all. What a lame ass! Jeffrey was too young to understand it, but my family was pretty pissed. How could he just walk away and not even bother to see his son?

CHAPTER THIRTEEN

I turn on the news and the first thing they are talking about is domestic violence. They act like this is something new. It has been around since the age of cavemen dragging their women around by their hair. Domestic violence is not just men hurting women. It's also women hurting men, same sex partners hurting each other, etc. It's a human versus human crime. It doesn't always come in the physical form. The emotional abuse can be even worse.

I know, because I've lived it. I could have died at his hands, but I didn't. At times, I wished I had died, but I'm glad I didn't. It's why I have to continue to write this book and share with you the experience of living through it and coming out a much better and stronger person. In all honesty, love is not worth the pain of going through any type of domestic abuse. That person DOES NOT understand what love is. Never again will I allow someone to put me in that position. Neither should you. Your life is precious, and there is no reason to sacrifice it by allowing someone to hurt you in any way.

Recently I decided to watch the movie *"The Burning Bed"* with Farrah Fawcett. I hadn't seen this movie in years and just felt the need to get my head back in the game after not writing for a week. The only person in her life, who saw things as they were, was her best friend. His family blamed her for everything, even though he was the one beating the hell out of her. Then he goes and lays a guilt trip on her to take him back after he gets into a car accident. She tried to stand her ground, and he continued to bully her until she had no choice but to kill him.

I've said it before, and I will continue to say it. I wish Mike had drawn my blood sooner. I don't condone physical violence at all, but if he had hit me hard enough to draw blood before he actually did, I wouldn't have reconciled with him. I may not have gotten pregnant with either child. I may not have lost my daughter. Who knows what would have happened? I just knew killing him would have cost me everything. I'm still here, and I do have a life outside of his bullshit. Now let's get back to the story.

Life was turning into a real struggle for me. I hadn't heard from Mike at all: no money from him for child support, to help pay the mortgage, lot rent or even to buy groceries. My parents suggested I go down to see if I could get some help from the state. I at least needed to get medical for my son. I was completely disgusted with how I was treated. This is what the caseworker told me word for word. "You're not black and you're not Mexican. There really is nothing I can do for you." What the hell is that supposed to mean? I am an American, and I pay my taxes like everyone else. I work my ass off, and this is what I get for it? I was 20-years-old with a two-year-old child. I barely made enough money to pay some of the bills. I wasn't getting any financial support at all from my son's father. They didn't give a shit about me or my son!

I felt so lost. I decided to keep looking for options. I had no choice. I had to survive for the sake of my son. I ended up getting a roommate, along with a couple of jobs, to help with the bills. It didn't work out too well with her, so she was gone after a couple of months. She was watching my son while I went to work at ASU. I found out she was inviting her boyfriend over to my home and having sex with him while she was supposed to be watching my son. Not only did the neighbors share this with me, but I found used condoms scattered all over the back bedroom that we shared. She would put Jeffrey in his room, or in the playpen, while she was intimate with her boyfriend. I wasn't having this crap anymore! I threw her ass out and with that, I was back to square one.

The bills kept mounting as things began to break down. I was having issues with the cooling and heating system in the house. Most of my money was going towards fixing it constantly. I made a choice to move back home with the folks and let the mobile home go. I never wanted to live in that tin box anyway. It was his choice. All those horrible memories needed to be out of my mind, and getting out of there did help. I decided that my job at ASU wasn't paying enough, so I went to work at a steel foundry just outside of town. I was making $8.50 an hour, and I could get the health insurance I needed for Jeffrey.

I finally heard from Mike. He wanted a divorce. I told him, since I didn't have the money to pay for it, he needed to be the one to file. That was a big mistake on my part! I should have found a way to pay for it. I will never forget the judge asking him if he wanted me to pay him spousal support. What the hell was that all about? Just because he filed for the divorce, let's not forget, AT MY REQUEST, he was allowed to get support from me? I don't think so! Especially since he hadn't made any effort to pay the mortgage, the lot rent or even child support. Screw that! I made sure to bring this up to the judge. They ordered him to pay $124 a month in child support. I was glad it was over, but it definitely wasn't the end of the bullshit.

Just because a judge orders child support to be paid, doesn't mean jack shit! I wasn't getting anything at all. Did I care? At this point, I gave up expecting any help from him what-so-ever. I couldn't count on him to give a damn about his own son's welfare. Hell, he didn't even bother seeing his child, or taking him for any type of visitation.

It wasn't long until I was faced with going back to court again. To this day, that son of a bitch blames me for all of this. I guess what he doesn't realize is, that I didn't continue dragging him into court. The Department of Economic Security did. When you don't make your child support payments, they tend to keep after you.

Well, things got worse this time, because he actually threatened me in court. Yes, right in front of the judge and everyone else! He was pissed off, because the judge was going to send him to jail for not making his payments. He acted all cocky and couldn't give a good enough reason as to why he hadn't been making his payments. So with that, the judge told him he was going to be spending a little time behind bars.

As they went to handcuff him and take him into custody, he said, "I'm gonna fucking kill you when I get out of here, bitch!" I was amazed to say the least! I never thought he would ever be that bold, or stupid, to say something in front of so many witnesses, much less officers of the law. What a dumb ass!

I felt on top of the world when they hauled him away into the back and out the door. It didn't take long before the judge spoke up on my behalf, and said he was going to issue an order of protection. I know those things don't stop someone, if they really want to hurt you, but in this case, it did help. I knew how much Mike despised going to jail and figured he wouldn't do anything to go back once he got out.

I remember a time when we were dating, and he ended up getting arrested. It was all kind of silly, to be honest, and it could have been avoided. We were hanging out on Microwave Mountain, and the cops showed up. He had just finished smoking a joint and didn't have any alcohol with him. The cop gave him a citation for no front license plate on his car. Back then it was illegal.

He blew off his court date. A short time later, we were with some friends when the car we were in broke down. We were in Victory Acres, a well-known area in Tempe for not being the nicest part of town at night. We had to push the car back to the house. The guys had a shotgun inside the open trunk, just in case anything happened.

Something happened all right. The cops came by with their lights on. We were told to pull the car over to the side of the road.

They weren't too happy to learn about the shotgun in the trunk. That wasn't the big deal of the night, though. They ran all of us through the system, and the only one who didn't come back clean was Mike.

They had no choice but to take him into custody, since he had a warrant out for his arrest. This was all because he didn't show up for his court hearing for a missing front license plate. Again, what a dumb ass! I will never forget when he called me the next day. He needed money to get out, and he didn't have any. He asked me to get together the bail for him, so of course I did. I sold my television and a few other things in order to get it. Talk about being stupid! I should have just let him sit there, or let him ask someone else to bail him out. But this was back when things weren't so bad between us, in the very beginning.

There was several times where I found myself in and out of court over this whole child support thing. I never fought him for anything. It seemed as if the Department of Economic Security "DES" was hounding me just as much as they were him. Don't get me wrong, it's great they were going after a deadbeat dad, but did they have to disrupt my life all the time as well? It never solved the problem. He sold off everything he owned to his friends for $1, just to get out of having any money to pay for his kid. I couldn't afford to take time off to deal with this crap.

On one occasion, he saw me in the hallway of the court and made a gesture towards me. He made his fingers on his hand into a gun and pointed it at me, pretending to fire it. What a sick bastard! I was a little shaken up by it, but I didn't let him see that. I just turned my head and continued walking down the hallway. The next time I went to court, I had a friend of mine come with me, well sort of. He refused to let me go to court alone, because he was worried about me. Pete was a pretty big guy, 6'5" and about 350 pounds of pure muscle. That guy was built like a brick shit house, and you wouldn't want to mess with him, because he would tear you up big time!

I'll never forget the response Mike gave me when he saw us walking into the courtroom. "What, you scared? Brought your bodyguard with you, huh?" Pete just laughed and leaned in towards him saying, "That's right, asshole. Fuck with her, and see what happens to your scrawny ass." With that, he went over to his side and shut up. It was great to see someone put him in his place. But then again, fighting a man was never his style.

The next time I came back to court, Mike brought a guy with him. This guy was maybe a hair under 6 feet tall and had a bit of bulk to him. I guess you could say that the little chicken shit brought his own bodyguard this time. As Pete and I walked down the hallway towards the court, Mike and his bodyguard were shooting the evil stares in our direction, trying so hard to intimidate Pete. It wasn't working. Pete thought it was really funny, and made a comment as we got closer to them. "Aww, he brought a little friend with him. I must have scared him." How could you not laugh at that?

CHAPTER FOURTEEN

The hardest part about writing this book, is trying to keep everything in chronological order as the years go by. The younger years are easy to keep in order, but then once the divorce went through, so much happened, and it has been almost 30 years. Not that my memory has faded, or anything like that. I do remember it all like it was yesterday. There are just some things that happened that I can't quite pinpoint on the timeline. Those were crazy messed up times in my life. I was trying to find a way to survive on a daily basis, and raise my son on my own, with no help from his father. It's no wonder I find it hard to remember the day-to-day order of things.

Life went on for me. After we split up, I did everything in my power to try and get my daughter back. Once I got my head clear of him initially walking out on us before Christmas, I started looking around the house for the adoption paperwork. Since I packed up all of his crap and set it outside, he wasn't able to get back into the house to get any of it. Thank God for that.

I found the paperwork and began my journey to try and find her. I went down to the adoption agency and met with the case manager, along with several other people. I had to relive the ordeal, baring my soul and sharing the nightmare I had just lived through in losing my baby. They told me it was too late, and there was nothing I could do to get her back, at least through them.

I left there in tears and couldn't imagine giving up at this point. My next attempt was to find a lawyer and see what I could do. I had a friend whose wife was studying to be a paralegal at the time. She had an internship working at a law firm. I reached out to them, and she gave me some advice. She put me in touch with a lawyer at her firm for a consultation. They even took care of the fees for me. I was so grateful!

The meeting with the lawyer was very insightful. He consulted with a friend of his, who was a judge in the local court system, and gave me the lowdown on how things would go. I could sue the adoption agency, but most likely wouldn't get anywhere in getting her back. I would have to sue the adoptive parents for custody in order to do that. The judge told him that custody cases were already back-logged in the court system, and we were looking at a waiting list of three years before we could get on the docket. He also mentioned that, depending on the financial status of the adoptive parents, I may see myself in court for many years over this. Custody battles can get brutal, ugly, take forever and cost a huge fortune. Money was something I definitely didn't have.

The lawyer said to take some time and think about what I really wanted to do. I had a lot on my plate, being a young single mother, and I had no idea of the emotional shit storm I was about to face. I spent an entire week going through every scenario in my head. I would write it down and re-read it back to myself. The one thing I kept coming back to, was how it would be at least three years before I could get into court and even tell this all to a judge. Three years is a long time. Then who knows how much longer it would be before the whole thing would come to an end and I could actually hold my child in my arms once again.

This whole experience really fucked me up emotionally. In my heart, I felt I had to get my baby back, but at what cost? I needed to be there for my son and be a good mother to him. I couldn't sacrifice him in the process of trying to get his sister back in our lives. Then there was my baby girl to consider. No matter how much my heart ached for her, how could I rip a child away from the only home she had ever known? How could I not expect this child to resent me and be so messed up for me doing that to her? It was the hardest thing I ever had to face in my entire life, but I had to let her go.

How the hell do you move on from something like this when a part of you has been so maliciously ripped away? If it weren't for Jeffrey, I would have ended my life right then and there. He gave me the strength to pull myself up and survive this hell once more. I went back to the adoption agency and shared with them what my decision was. I explained that I was given the option by the attorney to sue them, but instead I made a deal with them. I asked for the sterilization surgery in exchange, and they agreed to it. So I had the tubal ligation done where I could no longer have any children. I still have no regrets about doing that to this day.

Several years later, there was a highly publicized case that ran across very similar lines to mine. It was known as the Baby Richard case in Illinois. The media outlets couldn't get enough of this case, and it was all over the news. We all got a front row seat to the tragic and brutal fight that ensued between the natural and adoptive parents. When I saw that precious little four-year-old boy being ripped away from the adoptive family and given back to the biological parents, it broke my heart. Those horrible screams coming from that child pierced a hole right in my soul. No one should ever have to live through something like that. Seeing this was even more validation for me that I did the right thing, no matter how much it killed me to do it.

Don't get me wrong. If I had known my little girl was living in a bad situation, I would have gone to the ends of the earth to yank her out of it. At that time, I didn't have a clue of what her life was like. I assumed she was in a good home, being raised by a great family who loved her. From what I've come to know over the past nine years, my daughter had a wonderful life growing up. Yes, I did eventually find her, but I have yet to still meet her in person.

How did I find her? It was a long and tedious journey, filled with one disappointment after another, and it started out like this. When I met with the staff at the adoption agency, as part of our agreement, they gave me the pictures in my daughters file. They were of her as a newborn and as an 18-month-old. They also agreed to keep the file open for her and let me send letters to her in case she ever looked for me. I found out later that they never kept them. I was so upset to learn this, since I wrote letters to her weekly for years.

When I got home, I took the pictures out, and I couldn't stop looking at them. I noticed white-out on the back of one of the photos. My curiosity got the better of me and I scratched it off. What I saw gave me a clue as to who she was. I now knew her name.

The worst thing about having a child out there, who you know is yours, is that you search the faces of every little girl you see and hope you find her. Anytime I would hear her name, I would turn and look to see if it was my little girl. Nope, it never was. It's a shitty feeling to know a part of you is missing, and you can't do a damn thing about it. The emptiness and ache never completely go away. It just subsides over the years, and you learn to let it go numb to deal with it. We kept her very much alive in our house through the years. Since both my son and daughter were born on the same day, a year apart, we would put two sets of candles on Jeffrey's birthday cake. His on one side, hers on the other. He would have the honor of blowing out both sets of candles.

I never hid the fact he had a sister. I didn't feel any reason to do so. I know he didn't fully understand things when he was little, but I would have never kept that kind of thing from him, no matter what. When he asked where his sister was, I would simply tell him she was out there somewhere with a family who loved her. As he got older, he asked me to tell him more. I shared some of the details with him, but once again, I didn't feel it was necessary to go into every ugly detail.

I searched for years under her last name. I even heard a rumor, from someone in my parent's church, that they knew who adopted her. It was supposedly a family here in Phoenix, which years later turned out to be untrue. I remember when this was mentioned to me, and how I went through every name in the phone book that resembled hers. I even got the balls to make a few phone calls to see if she was there. I was greeted with the all too familiar phrases. No, there was no one by that name or you have the wrong number. My heart would break just a little more each time I heard "NO," so I had to give up on that idea.

I found myself at a crossroads, and I did the only thing I really knew how to do to help get myself past it. I wrote about it. I ended up winning an award, and it was published in an international anthology. Let me share it with you.

Where is She Now?

I wonder...as I stare out the window...where is she now? The thoughts of her weigh heavy on my mind, day and night. My heart aches at the need to have her near me. Is she somewhere far away, or is she close enough for me to reach out and touch her? How does she look now? Is she tall or short, freckle-faced, long hair, short hair? Does she have a lot of friends? Has she had an enjoyable childhood, or has she endured pain and strife?

When I go places, I find myself searching the faces of little girls everywhere, hoping to catch one glimpse of my precious, little girl. Every time someone yells her name, I look fast to see if it's her.

Someday soon, I hope our paths will cross, and I can make the fantasy of seeing her become a reality. It's a fantasy I find myself relishing in almost daily.

Oh how I long to be with her, hold her in my arms, tell her how much I've missed having her in my life, expressing my love for her, seeing how she's grown and experience the love of a daughter.

I know I may never have this, but it's nice to dream. I will always love you my little Lynsey... Mommy will always love you.

Through the years, I continued to search for her on the internet, but always came up empty. Many years later, 2005 to be exact, I was working at Metro Networks as a Producer/Reporter. It was at the tail end of my morning shift that I had an amazing thing happen. It was the day of my son's 20th birthday and my daughter's 19th birthday. I decided to put her name into the Google search bar, and the usual things came up, including images. I saw something that really floored me, and I had to hit on that image. Once I got a bigger and clearer view, the tears came streaming down my face. Our resident sweetheart, Dani, came over to me and asked me what was wrong. I remember those words so clearly now. "I think I just found my daughter." The resemblance was so uncanny, that it was simply mind blowing! I felt as if I was looking at a reflection of myself in a mirror.

Once I got past the tears to see a little clearer, I noticed this picture was on her website. She was an artist. I then noticed I was off on the spelling of her last name by one letter. Just one letter had kept me from finding her all these years. ONE DAMN LETTER! I've always been a believer in fate, and figured it was meant to happen at this time for a reason. I couldn't believe it! Dani hugged me, and eventually the rest of the staff found out what had just happened.

Before I left the building, I made a call to my son. I wished him a very happy birthday and said I had a present for him. I told him I had just found his sister.

CHAPTER FIFTEEN

Sometimes I feel like a soldier who has lived through many wars and battles. I can never tell someone who has been on the front lines fighting, that I know how they feel. I don't. I can understand it and relate to it in some ways, but I can never fully grasp the horrors they have lived through, and continue to, once they come home. I've had my own hell I've lived through, and the flashbacks can be brutally painful at times. Continuing on the journey of writing this book is exactly that, reliving those times through flashbacks. It's the only way I can remember a lot of the details I share with you.

I was a huge fan of *The Equalizer* TV show back in the late '80s. Edward Woodward's portrayal of a bad ass with a heart, really struck a chord with me. I was glued to that show every week. I had to see Robert McCall come to the rescue and deliver his brand of karmic justice. Oh, how I wished he would show up on my doorstep and save me from my daily hell. He never did.

I recently saw the Hollywood movie version of *The Equalizer*, and wasn't sure they could pull it off. I was once again thrown back into that world of karmic justice, and Denzel Washington definitely captured the true essence of what I remember best about the show I was so passionate about.

All throughout the movie, I found myself feeling more and more invigorated about writing this book. Why, you may ask? It's simple really. I kind of feel like "The Equalizer." I am no bad ass, like the character on the TV show or the film, but I certainly feel like I can deliver my own brand of karmic justice, and not only kill off my own demons, but help many others to banish theirs in the process.

When all of this crap happened in my life back then, I wasn't strong enough to stand up and fight for myself. But you can bet your ass that over time, I became a much stronger person, and there is no way I am going to let those demons, one person in particular, tear my life to shreds once again. I can only hope my daughter doesn't fall prey to him.

Living with a sociopath in your life is never an easy thing, especially when you don't know that person is one. Even when you end the daily relationship with them, it seems as if they always find a way to stay in your life. After we split up, I found out through my brother, that Mike was asking him questions about who I was seeing, and what I was doing in my life. What the hell business was it of his? He had no right to know. If he had taken an active role in being a father, then I can understand why he would have an interest in who was around in my life, for his son's sake. That wasn't the case at all. It was all about knowing every detail, so that he could try to find a way to control my life from the outside. How fucked up is that?

I told my brother to keep his damn mouth shut and not say anything to Mike about my life. You would think he would want to protect his sister, but Mike had conned him in a way too. Mike was there when he had the accident at the lumber yard. They also shared the garage enclosed room in my parent's house for a short time. I'm sure they bonded in a way, and Mike saw this as his ace in the hole when it came to having that forever looking glass into my life from afar.

I was doing my best to move on with my life. I had a good friend, who felt it was time I got back into the dating world. She said I needed to meet a good guy, who could be there for me and be a positive influence on Jeffrey. I don't know why most people feel you need a father and mother at home for kids to grow up right. I think, and in fact I know, this is bullshit. I raised a very well-adjusted, wonderful human being, who turned out to make his mother very proud. Fuck not having a father while he grew up. He calls me his MAD- Mother and Dad. You bet I love that!

Anyway, I was invited out to a picnic, and I ended up meeting this guy named Gary. He was very charming, and within a few weeks, we were dating. After a while, we decided to move into a place together. At that time, Gary and Jeffrey got along amazingly well, so I had no worries about moving to the next step. We eventually got married. It was nice to have someone around who didn't create any kind of problems and who seemed to love both my son and me. He was very protective of us. A girl could get used to that, especially after the shitty life I had just lived through with my former husband.

All through this time, Mike never came around, never called. He never bothered to come and see his son. He wasn't paying child support either. At this point, I really could have cared less. I just did what I had to every day to make sure I had food on the table for my family, and that Jeffrey knew his mommy loved him. Mike had moved on with his life as well. The details were always a bit surprising. It seemed that everyone else had to share things with me, no matter how many times I said I didn't want to know. I was just glad to not have him pulling his power trip shit on me and my life anymore.

He had been involved with several women, but the real kicker was that he got several of them pregnant. One of them was the woman of the married couple he moved in with after he left me: Debi. I'm sure this kid is not aware of his actual parentage, and Jerry has always denied the boy was Mike's. Not my problem to worry about. I had my own life to deal with. Eventually he ended up living with, and marrying, one of the other people in the group who used to hang out with us at Country Club and Southern: Sue. That's when things started to change.

Out of nowhere, I heard from Mike. He wanted to set up a visitation. Really? After all this time? I learned real quickly why. His new wife, Sue, had encouraged it. She was the one who pushed this to happen. Miraculously, my child support payments started coming in as well. If it weren't for her, I honestly don't believe he would have even bothered with his son. Future things proved that to be very true. Things started off okay for the most part, but within a short time, problems began to arise. I was having behavioral issues with Jeffrey every time he came home from a visit. He wouldn't listen to me at all. I had no idea what he was being exposed to over there.

On the last weekend visit with his father, I received a phone call from them. I was told that Jeffrey had possibly been bitten by something, maybe a spider. They weren't sure. They noticed that his body began to swell up. I can't remember if I went to pick him up, or if I asked them to bring him home. That part is a bit fuzzy to me. When I saw him, I was both scared and furious! His body had swollen so badly, that I was really worried.

I got him in to see a doctor and I will never forget what he said to me in his accusatory tone after the initial examination. "What kinds of drugs are you doing, young lady? I'm going to have to call CPS and report you for this." I was extremely pissed off at him! Mama bear came back at him with a fury in her voice. "He spent the weekend with his father, and it sure as hell didn't happen while he was with me. I don't appreciate you assuming that you know a damn thing about how this happened. Go ahead and report this to CPS, but get your story straight first before you do."

He was a little stunned, to say the least. His face had turned red, and I wasn't sure if that was from embarrassment, or because he was pissed at me for telling him off. I really didn't give a shit. I just wanted to make sure he wasn't going to make a false report and cost me my son. I would literally die if he did that! Losing one child was all that I could handle, but if you attempt to take my other child from me, be prepared for a fight, mother fucker!

It turned out that Jeffrey had an allergic reaction to the drug sulfa. It's in prescription medication which helps to treat things like a urinary tract infection. I found out Sue had to work that day, and Mike was supposed to be watching Jeffrey. Apparently he told Jeffrey to leave him alone and go play while he stayed in bed asleep.

Jeffrey told me that he climbed up on a chair and found an open bottle on the counter. He thought they were M&M's. Thank God he didn't swallow too many of them, or things could have been a lot worse!

That literally was the end of the weekend visits. CPS had been notified by the doctor, and they in turn told me I was not to let Mike see his son unless it was under some form of supervision. If I went against them, they would not only arrest him and file charges, but they would take my son from me and place him in foster care. I certainly wasn't having that. It's not like he even gave a damn anyway. It was his wife who wanted Jeffrey to come around. It's pretty sad that both she and I did everything we could to get him to take an active interest in being there for his son, but he just didn't give a damn.

Things were starting to go in a not so good direction in my own home. Gary began to have his young daughter come over for weekend visits. His ex-wife was a real piece of work. She would tell the kid to pump us for information and report things back to her. Why do parents think this is a good idea? Quit fucking with your kids mind like that, and be a real parent! You are supposed to have healthy relationships with your children after a divorce, not use them to carry out your vindictiveness, because your relationship ended with your spouse.

That wasn't even the worst part. His daughter started exhibiting really bad behavior and began creating problems with my son. She would claim Jeffrey was doing bad things when, in fact, she was doing them. She was, after all, daddy's little girl, and she was trying to make sure her daddy didn't forget it. We disagreed on the punishment, because he didn't bother getting to the bottom of the problem. He immediately took her side. I always tried to talk it out and see what really happened before we disciplined anyone. One time the truth came out and totally by accident. I overheard her telling Jeffrey she was going to break one of her toys and blame him for it. I wasn't having this crap anymore.

I went and got Gary from the living room. I told him to stand near the door and listen to what was going on. He was a bit stunned at what his daughter was saying. I think he finally woke up. It took him long enough. I made a decision to keep this from happening in the future. From now on, Jeffrey and I would go out for a while when he had his visitation. That way, he could spend more one-on-one time with her. She obviously felt threatened that her daddy was spending more time with Jeffrey than her. Problem solved for now, right? Not for long, because something new was about to fuck up my life once again.

CHAPTER SIXTEEN

In life, you have to take the good with the bad. Sometimes one bad thing can turn your life upside down, no matter how much good there is. Just when I thought I had found my protector, those tables were turned on me once again. There was a good thing that happened right before this, that had me confused when the bad incident happened. I couldn't understand why the quick flip. I understand it now. Allow me to explain, starting with the good.

During the weekend, Gary, Jeffrey and I went to a place called Tempe Sales. Gary needed some material for a project he was working on. When we rounded the corner of the aisle, we came face to face with my ex-husband Mike. I was very uncomfortable seeing him there. Of all the places in this big state he could be, why the hell was he here at the same time as we were? Well, he wasn't too happy to see me with Gary, by the look on his face. It was awkward as hell, but I had to introduce the two of them. Gary went to shake his hand, and you could see the tension in both of their faces, along with the strong gripping action going on in that handshake. I was expecting it to escalate to a good old fashion brawl. That wasn't Mike's style, though. He'd rather hit a woman.

Jeffrey was behind me, and he came closer to see the two guys shaking hands. He asked Gary who the guy was. Mike leaned down to him and said, "Do you remember me?" Jeffrey answered back, "Yeah, you're Mike, the guy with the Monte Carlo." Mike, the guy with the Monte Carlo? What the hell was that? Not, "You're my dad," or, "Hi, Daddy." WOW! I was speechless! My son had no idea this man before him was his daddy. It was pretty sad and pathetic that Mike didn't give a damn enough about his first born son to even make any kind of an impact on this kid as his daddy. He did spend the first two and half years with this kid when we were married, yet Jeffrey doesn't know him to be Daddy? You would have expected him to speak up and say "It's me, Daddy." Nope, didn't happen, and it didn't even seem to bother him!

I was floored to say the least! That handshake seemed to last quite a while, and Mike finally retracted from it. Both of their hands were red, like they had squeezed the life out of each other's. I was so thankful Gary was there with us. I didn't feel threatened by Mike's presence, but I really didn't feel good about him being there either. Even though my knight in shining armor was there to protect me that day, the ugliness in him was just brewing beneath the surface. It wasn't long until I got a taste of it, and so did my son.

We were married less than a year when I bore witness to what I call the "Jekyll and Hyde hell." Jeffrey was at the kitchen table coloring. Gary and I were in the living room with the TV on. I was busy doing some paperwork, and didn't pay a lot of attention to what was beginning to transpire. He was changing the channels, trying to find something to watch. He stopped on a channel that had Jeffrey's favorite show on. He turned up the volume slightly, and I noticed him looking over at Jeffrey. He turned up the volume again and looked over in his direction once more. This time Jeffrey got up from the table and came out to the living room to watch the show. That's when all hell broke loose.

Within a matter of minutes after Jeffrey sat down, Gary changed the channel. Jeffrey asked him why he had changed it, because that was his favorite show. Gary didn't say a word. He slapped his hand down hard across Jeffrey's face and sent him up about five feet and back down to the floor. Holy fuck! What did I just witness in my house? You can bet your ass that mama bear came out with a vengeance once again, and I ran to my son's side. I looked at his face and saw a red welt across it. I was fucking livid! "What the fuck do you think you're doing? How dare you hit my kid like that, you son of a bitch! I should fucking kill you for that! You need to get your shit and get the hell out of here...NOW!" I said with the fierce roar of a pissed off, protective mother. I was not about to stay with this man after what I had just witnessed.

He just sat there in his recliner. Sound familiar? I was about to call 911, and he decided to play fucking mind games with me. He kept telling me he was sorry, and he wasn't going to leave, because we needed to work it out. He said if I left him, he was going to kill himself. I took one look at him and laughed while I said this, "Go ahead and fucking kill yourself. It will be cheaper and easier for me than getting a divorce." Yes, I know, cold and callous, but can you blame me? After the hell I had lived through with Mike, I wasn't about to go through this shit again. I was not going to allow my son to be hurt like that and for no reason at all.

I called 911, and the paramedics showed up, along with the police. They checked Jeffrey over, and he seemed fine, other than being a little shaken up and the red welt on his face from Gary's hand. Gary just sat there in his recliner and started taking pills. Oh joy! *Do it, mother fucker, kill yourself. I dare you!* The cops would have hauled him off to jail for hitting Jeffrey, but they couldn't, since he claimed he was going to commit suicide. They had to take him to the nut house for a 72 hour evaluation period. At least he would be out of my home.

The officer told me they would have to take him to the hospital first in order to pump his stomach, since he had claimed to be taking pills to kill himself. They asked me if I had seen how many he had taken, and I said no. I was highly distracted by my son at the time, and I could have really cared less if he swallowed one, or the whole damn bottle, to be honest. They took him away in the ambulance, and the police car followed behind. I received a call a little while later from one of the officers, and he told me that Gary had only one pill in his stomach. Are you fucking kidding me? One lousy pill! So much for killing yourself, huh loser?

With Gary gone, I had to figure out what I was going to do next. I had two choices: pay the rent and stay there, or rent a U-Haul and get the hell out of there. I thought I could move back home until I could figure out what to do. I called my folks, told them what happened, and asked for advice on what to do. To be honest, that was one of the worst mistakes I ever made.

After everything I went through with Mike, you would have thought my dad would tell me to come home where it was safe for Jeffrey and me. He did no such thing. He told me to pay the rent and wait it out until Gary was released from the mental evaluation. I trusted my dad to steer me in the right direction, but he ended up telling me to do something I regret doing to this day.

So I paid the rent and decided to stay. What the hell was wrong with me? I guess I figured that, once he was released, we could talk it out like two civilized adults and go our separate ways. Of course, that didn't happen. Story of my life.

After the 72 hour evaluation was completed, they called and asked me to come down for a consult and to take him home. I wasn't sure what to expect. I had never been to the state mental hospital before. It was a weird experience I don't ever want to have again. It felt very cold and sterile the minute I walked into the door. It reminded me of the morgue.

During the consult, they said there was nothing wrong with him mentally. They said it appeared to be an act of desperation when he said he was going to kill himself. Okay, so now what? I was then taken into a room where I saw Gary sitting across the table from me. It felt very awkward to see him like that. He was very apologetic, and his face was full of tears streaming down. I didn't know what the hell was going on with him. This was the Gary I knew and loved, not the Gary who had hit my son. Talk about a serious mind fuck!

I took him home that night, and things seemed to be just fine for a little while. I'm sure you can guess by now that, once again, the shit was about to hit the fan, but in a way I could have never expected. We were all sitting in the living room watching TV. It was pretty quiet. Jeffrey was on the loveseat on one side of the room, and Gary and I were on the couch. I started to get cold, so I reached for the blanket.

I decided to lie down on the couch, because I was a bit exhausted. I hadn't slept much in the past few days with all that had happened. I had just taken a shower, so I was very relaxed. I began to fall asleep, and the next thing I know is that I'm being awakened by Gary underneath the blanket, in between my legs performing oral sex on me.

I tried pushing him off of me, but he wasn't lifting up. He kept pushing my legs down, and I couldn't move. Tears started streaming down my face as I continued to struggle. I kept telling him to stop, but he wasn't listening to me. I was trying so hard for Jeffrey not to see what was happening. He had already lived through enough trauma, and he didn't need to see this too. I finally managed to get one of my hands free, and I started punching Gary. That didn't seem to help, so then I started clawing him on the side of his face, and he finally got off of me.

He moved to the other side of the couch. I sat there, trying to compose myself for what seemed like an eternity. I finally got up and got Jeffrey off to bed. I made my way into the bedroom, wrapped myself up in my robe, grabbed my pistol, put it in my pocket and went to bed. I cried myself to sleep that night, with my hand inside my pocket holding on to the gun for dear life. If he tried to do that to me again, I would be prepared to end his life.

The next morning came, and I woke with my hand still tucked deep inside my pocket, holding the gun. I got up and didn't bother getting dressed. I wanted to make sure I kept that gun in my pocket and within reach, just in case I needed it. He didn't say much to me at first. Later in the day, he came over to me and tried to kiss me. I pulled away from him and he grabbed ahold of my arm. He whispered into my ear how much he enjoyed being home with me again, and that he was looking forward to making love later in the day. Are you fucking kidding me? After the shit you just pulled last night? I don't think so, pal.

I let him know there was no way in hell I would allow him to touch me again. Of course, I got the whole speech about how I was his wife, he loved me, and that we should make love. Again, are you fucking kidding me? Were you not the one who had just raped me the night before? Yes, performing oral sex on me against my will is RAPE! You love me? Fuck you, buddy!

"If you touch me again, I will fucking kill you! I will shoot you where you stand! Leave me the fuck alone! Stay away from me, or I will call the cops on you again!" I said with a vengeance just beneath my breath, so Jeffrey wouldn't hear me. He wouldn't listen, so I did just that. I called 911 again!

I held the phone in one hand and the gun inside my pocket in the other. I don't think he took me seriously at first, but I was about to show him he had fucked with me for the last time. I started telling my story to the 911 operator. "You guys were out here several days ago when my husband hit my son and then pretended to commit suicide. You guys hauled him off to the nut house, and now he is back at home. Last night he raped me, and he has intentions to do it again. You need to send an officer over here to get him out of my home before I kill him."

The operator asked me if I had a weapon. "Yes, I do have a gun, and I will use it if you don't come and get him out of my home. I'm not going to allow him to hurt my son and me ever again. Please send someone out here to get him out of my home." She told me to take my son and leave the apartment in order to go someplace safe. I told her I couldn't, because he was blocking the door, and he had the keys. She was trying to put me off on having an officer come out. She asked me if we could talk things through. I told her, "Hell, no! I'm done talking things through, and if you don't get someone out here now to remove him, you will be getting another call back to have someone come and pick up the damn body!" You think she took me seriously then?

It didn't take long before several officers arrived. One of them was an officer who was there the prior week, and he remembered what had happened. The second he walked in the door, I told him I had a gun in my pocket, and if he wanted me to give it to him, I would. He seemed to be more concerned about me and Jeffrey, asking if we were okay.

I told him Jeffrey was fine, but I wasn't doing so well. He asked me to tell him what was going on. I told him I had brought Gary home from the mental hospital last night, and he had raped me. I explained it all in detail, and how I slept with a gun in my pocket all night. I went on to tell him what had just taken place before they arrived.

He could see I was pretty distraught as I relived the events all over again for him to hear. He touched my shoulder and told me everything was going to be okay. He reassured me that Gary would leave the premises. His partner was busy talking to Gary and trying to keep him calm. He just kept telling the officer everything was fine, and I was overreacting. Seriously? Overreacting, my ass!

The officer, who was talking to me, told Gary he needed to pack up a few things to take with him and leave the apartment. He told Gary he had 10 minutes, and then they would escort him out. He tried to take control of the situation by telling them, "It's okay guys, you can leave now. I'm going to take a walk around the block and let her cool off. We can talk about this when I get back."

I was a bit floored by what he had just said. I wasn't going to let that happen. You are so out of here, mother fucker! "I don't want to talk about it anymore. He raped me last night and there is no way in hell we are going to work this out. Get him the hell out of here before I kill him!"

Once again, Gary persisted and told them he wasn't going to leave, because we would work it out. I pleaded with the one officer, and he now demanded Gary get an overnight bag together so he could leave. Amazingly enough, Gary said it one last time, about how we were going to work it out. They had enough of his shit and told him he had to leave NOW! He tried to put them off again by saying he would go pack up some of his stuff. They were DONE with his verbal bullshit games.

"You had your chance to pack your stuff up, and you chose to argue with us instead. Now it's time for you to leave. Let's go," the officer said very sternly as he led him out the door. You have no idea how awesome it felt to not only win the battle, but also the war.

CHAPTER SEVENTEEN

We've all heard what doesn't kill you makes you stronger, but damn, how much more of this shit was I going to have to go through in this lifetime? I was 22 at this point in my life, so I kept wondering what the hell was going to happen next. Was I going to be able to actually live a good, happy life from this point on? As usual, I kept being tested, but I learned I could handle whatever life had to throw at me next.

I was very thankful Gary was now out of our lives. Well, sort of. I still had to get a divorce, and that sure wasn't easy. He called me a couple of days after the police made him leave. He had made his way up to Prescott and was staying with his aunt and uncle. He begged me to let him come home, and I threatened to hang up on him. There was no way in hell I was about to let him come back into our lives and cause any more harm. If there was one thing I took from the previous hell I lived through, it was not to remain in a relationship with anyone who exhibited that kind of behavior towards my son and me.

I told him I wanted a divorce, and I would be sending him the paperwork later that week. He said he wasn't going to give me one, and he wanted to work it out. Again, I made sure he heard me loud and clear. "There is no way in hell I will ever let you step foot in my home, or my life, ever again! You need help, and I'll be damned if Jeffrey and I are going to pay the price for your bullshit!" As was his usual style, he continued on with his ranting, saying I was his wife, he loved me with all his heart, and he wouldn't let me go. I slammed the phone down into the receiver. End of conversation. You don't get to decide, mother fucker! That is my choice!

I went down to the courthouse the next day and filed the paperwork. I sent it off with all the legal stuff to prove it was delivered. I couldn't believe it was that easy, but I was wrong once again! The universe has always challenged me, and it wasn't about to stop now. Within a few days, the papers came back as undeliverable. He was no longer at their house, and he had taken off. I made several phone calls to them, but they never answered the phone. I found out a few days later, he had left the state and moved back home to Arkansas. So much for getting my divorce from this bastard!

I wasn't giving up just yet. I knew there was a way to do this, especially since I had police records to show the recent incidents and what he had done. I didn't even have to go to the extent of using them. All I had to do was publish it in the local newspaper for 90 days, to see if he would respond. He didn't even bother to respond or show up in court, so the judge granted my divorce. I was free of this asshole, but then I had to deal with the other one who was in my life prior to this. It never ends, does it?

I was married to Gary for less than a year when all this shit happened. In between this time, I had to deal with something that surfaced with Mike. He left me a voice mail one day, saying he wanted nothing to do with Jeffrey anymore. He wanted to give up any rights to him. I was a bit surprised by this call, because it came out of the blue. I hadn't heard from him in a while, and then I get this kind of message. Can you guess why?

After I got this message, I went to the court and spoke to someone about how I could relinquish his parental rights to my son. I didn't want to have to go back to court and see him again. She suggested I type up a statement and have him sign it in front of a notary. Once I got it, then I could file the legal paperwork and attach the document to it. She said I wouldn't even have to face Mike in court. Wow! Really?

I typed up a document the way I was told to, and I even went one step further. I not only put on there about relinquishing his parental rights, but I also stated he wouldn't have to pay child support anymore. It's not like he was paying it anyway. Come to find out, the reason why he wanted to give up his rights was because he thought he wouldn't be on the hook for the support if I agreed to all of this. Honestly, I didn't give a rat's ass about the support anymore, because I was tired of how many hours and days I wasted being back in court dealing with this shit, thanks to DES. We both found out later that apparently, you can't get out of paying your child support, even if your rights are relinquished.

I called him back and we agreed to meet at the bank at Country Club and Southern. My dad drove me to the meeting, since he had an account there, and the notary would be free. I really didn't want to see Mike, but if it meant putting an end to his reign of terror in my life, and never having to deal with him again, it was well worth it. I was in shock, just as everyone else was at the bank that day. He signed that piece of paper just like it was the title to a used car he was selling. He threw the pen down on the counter and just left the building, and like that, my son, his first born son, was mine 100%. (See document at the end of the book.)

Just because I obtained full rights to my child, didn't mean I was done dealing with his biological father. I sincerely wish I was, but when you meet up with a sociopath, you never truly get away from them. They haunt you throughout your life like the fucking plague! I was beginning to think there was something truly wrong with me, to not only attract someone like Mike, but also someone like Gary. You would have thought both of them were cut from the same cloth, but they weren't. Neither one of them could let me go, or leave me alone. What the hell was wrong with these two assholes? Didn't they understand the real meaning of letting go and moving on? Apparently not!

Gary's issues were different than Mike's. I found out several years later, that Gary was bi-polar and should have been taking medication. He wasn't taking anything when we were together. It was the reason why he would flip like a switch and have those outbursts from hell. Honestly, I don't think I would have even taken him back in my life if he had gotten the medication shit all figured out. Too little, too late, buddy! The damage had already been done.

He tried reaching out to me every year for five years in a row. He would call my mom's house, because he knew we all gathered there on Christmas Eve. He tried like hell to get me back each time.

"I still love you. We need to be together. My heart belongs to you." Blah, blah, blah. I remember the very last call he ever made to me. He was now living in Tennessee, and wanted me to go out there to be with him. "There's only one problem though, you would need to get rid of your concert t-shirts and moccasins," he said. "I'm gonna get you a cowboy hat, some nice jeans and boots that will look great on you."

Um, who the fuck do you think you are, my daddy? There is no way on God's green earth you are going to change what I wear. I could not believe what I was hearing! At this point in my life, I was wearing business suits and dresses, because I worked in television and radio. Sure, I still wore my concert t-shirts once in a while, because they were comfortable. I made it known to him that, any chance he may have had in reconciling with me, was just squashed. There is NO fucking way I am going to be forced to wear something to fit into your world, buddy. I have my own style, and if you don't like it, you can kiss my ass!

It didn't seem to affect him at all. I wasn't expecting what came next. "Oh, and I have to kind of explain the situation I'm in right now. I have a roommate, and I also live with my daughter," he said. "Floretta?" I asked. "No, I have another daughter," he said. "The roommate is her mother." Are you fucking kidding me? Here we go again. "Okay, so this is your wife, or girlfriend, and you have a kid with her?" I asked. "No, she is a friend who desperately wanted a baby, and she asked me to be the father of it," he continued on. Okay, so I decided to play along. "So, you donated your sperm, and she was artificially inseminated?" I asked. "No, she didn't want to do it that way. She wanted it to be natural," he said.

"Okay, so you fucked her then," I said. "No, it wasn't like that. I just helped her make a baby, like she wanted, that's all," he said. I'm sure you can imagine what I was about to say. "So you really think I was born yesterday, asshole? Seriously? You fucked her many times in order to get her pregnant. You weren't a fucking sperm donor. She was, and is, your girlfriend, and you're fucking her all the time, and oops, out pops a baby. Geez, you could have been a little bit more creative than that. I may be blonde, but I'm certainly not fucking stupid." With that, I told him I was done with his bullshit games, and from this point on, I would not be answering the phone at my parent's house during the holidays. He could go fuck himself and his girlfriend too!

It wasn't long after Gary and I split up that I began dealing with the other wolf at my back door yet again. A very good friend of my brother's, Loy, was killed in a tragic accident. Loy was one of those good-looking country boys, who had just begun to strike a chord in the entertainment industry as an actor. This guy was going places, and we expected him to become a big Hollywood movie star someday, but he never got the chance. He was one of our ushers when Mike and I got married. At the time of Loy's death, Mike and Sue were married. She also knew Loy and was part of the group who hung around with him.

The day of the funeral arrived. Our 25-year-old friend was to be laid to rest, while we all paid tribute to his sweet soul. You would think that the asshole Mike would leave his crap at the door before he set foot into the church, but nope, he didn't. He came alone. No wife by his side. What was up with that? She would have wanted to be there. Loy was her friend and not really Mike's. So where the hell was she?

I've been to many funerals in my lifetime, but this one was the most awkward ever. The entire time I was trying to listen to the service, I could feel someone's eyes on me. I'm sure you know that creepy type of feeling. I looked out the side of my eye several times and could see Mike staring at me. He should have been paying attention to the service, but he just sat there looking at me. What the fuck is your problem, buddy? I'm not the only one who noticed this. Several people brought it up to me after the service. I was hoping he would leave and not follow us to the graveside ceremony.

I left the church and headed out to my car. Just as I was about ten steps away, there he was. He followed me out to the parking lot. Oh shit, now what? He tried to touch my arm, but I pulled it away fast. He said he just wanted to talk to me. "You look great. I really like that dress on you. It makes you look sexy," he said. "How about we go somewhere to talk and get something to eat." Are you fucking kidding me? Are we really standing here at a funeral, and you're hitting on me? Not on your life, asshole! He asked me once again, and all I could say was, "Hey, where's your wife? Where's Sue? I thought she was good friends with Loy? How come she's not here with you?" I don't think he expected me to come back with those questions by the look on his face.

As he moved closer toward me, I opened up the car door and started to get in. He tried to talk to me, but I took the upper hand once again. "Go home to your wife. I have a graveside service to attend." With that, I slammed the door and left. I found out a few years later what had happened, and why Sue was not there. He apparently beat her up and locked her in a closet. I can't tell you any more details. I wasn't there, and it is her story to tell, not mine. It's a real shame this asshole continued to destroy people's lives and left the carnage that he did, and yet, we all survived.

CHAPTER EIGHTEEN

Being a survivor is nothing to feel glamorous about. It's really a harsh term when you think about how we earn it. So many people fall prey to those who victimize. I sit here working in my office, and once in a while I turn on the TV for background noise. I'm not a regular viewer of Dr. Phil, but as of recently, I have seen several of his shows that have caught my interest. They are about domestic violence and young girls in relationships with much older men who are abusive. Are you fucking kidding me? This is the 21st century, and this shit is still going on! You would think that these girls would have a clue.

The 16-year-old is dating a 29-year-old man. She has no father in her life, only her mother. It comes out during the interview that her mother was abusive towards her, and she wonders why her daughter fell into the hands of an abusive man. Wake the hell up, people! What you put your children through while they are growing up will make them fall prey to this kind of abuse, because they think it's normal. They don't have a clue as to why you are protesting now, when all they are used to is the abuse from a very young age.

Then you have the 18-year-old girl who gets pregnant by the 30-year-old guy. He's been in and out of jail for numerous things. Her parents are actually fighting for her, but she is so "in love" with this guy, and she can't stay away from him. They purposely get her pregnant, so her parents will be forced to accept him. If they don't, they won't be allowed to see their grandchild. Again, you've got to be fucking kidding me!

I understand how they can be so lost and clueless. I can honestly say this as someone who has lived through this kind of shit and who has had years to get past my ordeal. The lack of education for these young girls is just insane! We need more victims to come forward, ban together and tell their stories. We need to educate the young while we can, in order to make a difference in this world.

I truly love the father on the second show. He's talking to his daughter and asking her if this guy has threatened to kill her if she leaves him. She is telling her father he has, in fact, threatened her with her life. His answer was, "I don't fear this guy. I don't fear him." I only wish my father could have been more like this and stuck up for me when he needed to.

It took me a few years to figure out that it's all about the fear. I had to live through it in order to learn that. Our young girls today shouldn't have to go through this. Even young men shouldn't have to experience this. With all of the stuff we have readily available through the internet, you would think that we would be a more educated society. Why do we as humans, have to continue to fall prey to these people who hurt and abuse? Can't we all work together to get this shit under control?

This is what abuse is about: control. Some people think, once you are involved with them, they have the right to tell you what to do. Last time I checked, we are in America, and we do have certain freedoms. I know in other countries, people aren't so lucky. Rules of control are in place, and women have to do as they are told by their husbands. I grew up in a house where my mother did pretty much everything my father told her to do. It wasn't the best atmosphere for me to be in, since I grew up believing I had to "obey" my husband. I always hated that damn word obey. It was part of the wedding vows for the longest time. You can bet your ass I wouldn't allow it to be part of any wedding vow I make nowadays.

I've also noticed a few things about myself, since I began this journey to talk about my life and my experience with domestic abuse. I tend to swear quite a bit, and my nerves are very raw. No matter how strong we are, and no matter how hard we fight, those scars always stay with us. I've never been one to shy away from being blunt, and I pity the idiot who says the wrong thing to me now. I still have somewhat of a filter in place, but not as much as I should. Unfortunately, in the human language, swear words tend to give us power. Why? I don't know for sure. Maybe it's the way we express ourselves while using these words that takes on the power for us. Our abusers sure know how to lay it on thick with those words when they brutalize and terrorize us.

In this book, I will never change the dialogue as it happened. I will not clean it up for anyone. If I did, the story would not resonate with other victims who have gone through the abuse. As a survivor, I've run across many others who have shared their stories with me. We have to find a way to empower ourselves, and in speaking to many others who have been victims, I've learned that we all tend to gravitate toward one swear word in particular: fuck. That word can take on so many meanings, but when it comes to survival, it's my expressive word, and I have no problem saying it if I feel the need to.

It was the most powerful word I spoke on the day I took the power away from Mike. I certainly wished I had learned to use it sooner. If I had, I probably could have avoided a lot of the bullshit I went through. Now keep in mind, it doesn't always help to exercise that wonderful word, and in some cases, it could cause the abuse to get a lot worse. You just have to figure out when it's the right time to use your power word to work for you.

CHAPTER NINETEEN

Through the years, I've had so many people ask me how I was able to get past all of this and move on to better things. To be honest, I stopped thinking about it and just started doing it. I concentrated more on being there for my child and raising him to the best of my ability. Having Jeffrey in my life gave me structure, purpose and direction. I didn't need to worry about Mike or Gary being able to get back into my life whenever they wanted. It would have been my choice to take either one of them back, and there was no way in hell I would have done that, given what the both of them had put me through.

I toughened up, and I guess you can say I grew ovaries of steel. Guys refer to it as growing a set of balls.

I worked any and all odd jobs I could to survive; landscaping, climbing huge palm trees and trimming them, foundry work, maid, merchandising, masseuse, etc. I even went back to college, finished my broadcasting degree, and set out on a course to become a much stronger person than I could have ever imagined. I took on the role of mother and dad. It's why my son affectionately calls me his MAD. God, I love that term! Don't get me wrong, it took a lot of work to become stronger. I went through several other things, which could have destroyed me in the process, yet I survived. One such experience almost landed me in jail, and could have cost me my son, thanks to my father.

Although I was starting on a new path of independence and strength, I still allowed my father to derail me. It damn near ended any chance of me having a decent life. Not a lot of people know this part of my past, but it is public record. I don't hide from it either. I can honestly say, if I had been strong enough at the time, I would have told my father to go to hell with the idea of what he was asking me to do. I was living back at home and paying rent. Yes, my father was charging rent for Jeffrey and me to live there. I was trying everything I could to put myself out there in radio, but it wasn't that simple. The job I had been promised at a local rock station was no longer available after I graduated. The program director had moved on, and it left me with no choice but to find whatever gig I could get.

I had to drive far distances and work outside of the valley, in order to start building a name for myself all over again. Most of the time in the radio business, you have to leave the state and work all over the country in order to build your career. I couldn't leave Arizona, because I had to make sure my son grew up around his family and not in some strange place. I thought I had struck gold with my first gig up in Payson at an oldies station, but it didn't last as long as I would have liked. We were all let go, because the station was switching to satellite programming with no live jocks locally. At that time, I was also working part-time for a local cable TV show as the promotions director and as an assistant editor and writer for a local music publication. Both of those were non-paid jobs.

I was on to my next job in Coolidge at a country station. It was a full-time gig, working six days a week. I also started doing massage again, to earn more money so we could get our own place. I began looking for an apartment I could afford. I found a two bedroom place in a four-plex off of Mesa Drive and Broadway. It wasn't too bad. My mom gave me some of her furniture, and I picked up a few used things. I spent some time fixing it up and making it a home for us. I was finally getting somewhere, but life was about to change yet again.

I had been at the station for about six months, when things took a bad turn. There came a time when the station wasn't paying us on-air jocks. We were being told that they were waiting on receiving payments from some of the clients. We kept getting promises from management, but nothing was happening. As most people in radio know, you stick it out, and don't walk away from a gig while you are trying to establish yourself, but this shit went on for five weeks! I was only making $4.25 an hour at the time. Yes, minimum wage. Not all radio personalities make the big bucks.

The jock, who was on the air before me, decided to stage a takeover and let everyone know we had been coming to work with no pay all this time. He drug me into it, and stuck around during my shift, bantering with me and the listeners about our woes. We played requests other country stations would play, but weren't on our playlist. We had listeners in the station with us, and people in the parking lot cheering us on. The sheriff's deputies, who were our fans, showed up to make sure that we weren't holding any hostages. They had received phone calls from people who misinterpreted what we had said which was, "We were holding the station hostage." They just laughed and joined in the fun with us. The *Arizona Republic* even did an article on us and what we had done. It didn't make the management move any faster in getting us our pay, and they took us off the air in the meantime.

I was scared and didn't know what I was going to do. I barely had any money in the bank, and now this. I started going through what little bit of personal stuff I had and tried to sell things, just to pay the rent. I was barely getting by, and I wasn't sure how I was going to even pay for food. I decided to ask my folks for advice on what to do. I was hoping for some guidance, but my father instead told me to apply for financial help from the state. I wasn't sure I would even qualify after what the lady had told me the first time I went in there. I picked up the forms and went over to my folks for dinner that night.

I sat at the kitchen table and began to fill out the paperwork. I didn't know how this stuff worked. I was way too young, and didn't have any knowledge of the welfare system, other than being told no when I really needed help the first time. I felt defeated and unsure of what to do. One of the questions referred to whether or not I had a job. I told my dad I didn't think I would qualify for help, since I had a job. He told me several times to check the no box. His reasoning was, "You're not getting paid anyway, so you don't really have a job." My eyes welled up with tears, and I just remember saying to him over and over again, "But I do have a job. What if they find out I'm lying? I can't lie like that." You would have thought he would agree with me and let it go. Nope, he didn't. He kept saying that

Jeffrey and I needed help, and since I wasn't getting paid, the state should help me. I allowed him to pressure me into telling a lie, and with that, I made a big mistake I can never take back. A few years later, it caught up to me.

A sheriff's deputy knocked on my door and served me with paperwork. I had to go down to the local jail and have my fingerprints taken, then I was to report to a private room in some office building for questioning regarding a potential fraud charge. I was never so scared in all my life! There were two people dressed in dark suits: a woman and a man. She seemed nice, while he ripped at me the whole time I was there. I realized I was being interrogated in a good-cop bad-cop type of situation. I told them the whole truth about the job situation, the form, my dad telling me to fill it out a certain way etc. The man wasn't buying it. He just kept yelling at me that I was ripping off the government, and I was lying about it. He said what I did was intentional. I was terrified, and tears were streaming down my face. I had never done anything like this and had no idea what was going to happen to me.

The next few weeks were hell for me. I had only received help from the state for five months, yet that one lie created so much guilt and fear, it nearly destroyed me. I was formally charged with a crime and given an attorney by the state to represent me. I was never arrested, nor did I spend any time in jail, thank God. I had a meeting with my attorney and told her everything I had shared with the two investigators. She told me, the best thing to do was plead guilty to a lesser misdemeanor charge and take a deal from the state to avoid going to jail. She said she didn't think it would be a problem, because I was a single mom and had never been in trouble with the law before. What was I supposed to do in this case? I had to take responsibility for what I'd done, even though my father had put me up to it. Ultimately, I said no on that form, and this is where it got me.

On December 19, 1994, I stood in the courtroom face to face with the judge. I felt so much fear and was worried that he wouldn't accept the deal the state had offered me. He said he was going to make an example out of me. I feared the worst was about to happen. He said people like me deserved jail time, but since I had made a deal with the state, he couldn't give me any. He decided to add something else to the deal. Honestly, as long as I didn't go to jail, I was fine with whatever he gave me. I had to pay for what I did, regardless of how it happened. I understood the line between right and wrong, and I had crossed it.

I was ordered to pay restitution of triple the amount, be on probation for three years, and to do 300 hours of community service. Since I was out of an actual job at the time, I decided to put all my effort into doing my community service as quickly as I could. I went through the list of places where I could do my service, and much to my surprise, the local PBS TV station allowed people to fulfill their obligation there. I had mixed feelings about it, but it was a world very familiar to me. I met with the volunteer coordinator, and she put me to work six hours a day, five days a week. I did everything possible at the station, fulfilling my community service in the marketing department within 10 weeks.

I was making payments to the court of $50 a month, along with my probation fees. Doing massage part-time allowed me to continue to pay this and put food on the table. The volunteer coordinator, who I had worked under, left in the middle of my community service, so I was handed over to someone new. She eventually offered me a job at the station after my service was completed. I was stunned! She told me, "You are such a hard worker, have a great personality, you work so well with everyone, and you know damn near everything there is to know around here. We would be foolish not to hire you." You can't imagine how overjoyed I felt when she said that to me. I had never been recognized for anything before, and it felt so wonderful to have someone on my side for a change.

Through this whole experience, I learned one thing more than anything: I could never look to my father again for any advice, whatsoever. His advice was toxic and hurt me far beyond what I could have ever imagined. I did something I would have never done, but for his prompting. That really scared the hell out of me! I understand it more now than I did back then. I don't like it when people play the victim and blame everyone else for their problems. Yes, my dad did, in fact, play a major role in this whole thing, but I did have to come to terms with the fact that I put that pen to that paper and checked that "no" box. It was on me, not him. To this day, he still takes no responsibility in giving me that advice, and to be honest, I really don't care anymore.

CHAPTER TWENTY

It seemed like my life was always one test after another. It still continues to this day, but not to the level it was back then. I couldn't understand why I had to face so many things at such a young age. You always hear things from people like, "God never gives us more than we can handle." Okay, maybe so, but why did God feel the need to test me over and over with these things? Was I not strong enough yet? You would have thought by now that I was done for a while with all of this. Not so.

I had experienced so many deaths in my life over an 11 year period, when I was 23-34. I lost everyone from friends to family members: 41 in all. They ranged in age from 23 to 65. I found myself going to more funerals than I would have liked to at this age. Put yourself in my shoes for just a minute. How would you feel, when someone new meets you and they make a comment like this: "I'm not sure if I should be friends with you. It seems death loves you quite a bit." Ouch, that really hurts. I wrote something back then to capture how I was feeling. Please allow me to share it with you.

The Grim Reaper Blues

You've invaded my life once again and spewed out your distasteful venom. You strike ever so quickly, grabbing your next unsuspecting victim, and tearing them away from me, and out of my life forever.

What gives you the right to mess with the lives of those closest to me? Why can't you go after someone else, and make them feel the hurt the way you inflict it upon me? It doesn't make any sense to me as to why I have to lose so much. I am not a bad person, so why do you insist on taking away all the people in my life? How many more times do I have to suffer this loss, thanks to you?

You think you are scaring me? You used to scare me, you really do nothing but anger me now. Quit pulling people away from me and taking them to a place beyond where I can't see or touch them anymore. I am tired of looking at pictures and memorials from the many services I have attended through the past years. I am not ready to go beyond this earth in order to see these people again. For now, you can continue to barrage me with your wrath.

Just know one thing, I am stronger for all the hurt you've put me through, and I will not leave here without a fight. I don't have many people left in my small, cherished circle, so go away and leave me be. Target someone else who doesn't appreciate life and people as much as I do. You have destroyed things long enough, and I can't let you do it any longer. I will fight till my last breath to keep a hold on those left in my life. There are too few precious people left, and I won't let you take them from me. I will continue to grow stronger every day, in case I have to do battle with you again. I will not lose my fight.

To make matters worse during this time, I had to deal with a new boss coming on board at the TV station. She made my life a living hell for many years, until I left in 2001. She was kind of a shut-off person to begin with and not very friendly to anyone. She wasn't at the station very long when the big fiasco happened.

It was during the December pledge drive. Things were fine the first two weeks of pledge, but as we got closer to Christmas, something went wrong and it took over six weeks to get to the bottom of it. Several of the shows did really well and brought in a ton of money for the station. Someone had decided to add extra viewings of the shows just a couple of days before Christmas.

These shows had premiums or "gifts" attached with a guaranteed Christmas Eve delivery. The breaks that were numbered to go along with these shows were all mixed up. People ended up getting the wrong premiums, and some never got theirs at all. It was a major pain in the ass for us in the marketing department. I had to bring in extra crews to go through all the pledges, call people, find out what they originally wanted and then make sure to get them the right gift by Christmas Eve as promised. Several staffers even took their own vehicles and personal time to make sure the correct gifts got to the homes of the viewers who had pledged for them.

Then we had the financial stuff to take care of. It took me several weeks to iron out all the details, but we finally did it. When the boss lady came in to talk to me about what I had found, I told her this, "We've got everything fixed now, and all the figures are balanced." She said, "So, what was the problem? What caused it?" I told her, "I'm not sure whose idea it was to add all of those extra breaks at the last minute, but that is what caused the problem." She said, with a nasty tone as she left the room, "It was my idea." Oh shit, now I I've done it. I just pissed off my new boss with my brutal honesty.

I sucked it up, took a deep breath, collected myself and a few minutes later, I walked into her office. I apologized to her, and said I didn't mean to upset or offend her. I was just being honest. I never realized telling the truth that day would cost me so much over the next several years. She bullied me in every way you could think of and without getting her own hands dirty in the process. She had my main supervisor keeping tabs on me, listening to my phone calls and counting how many times I went to the bathroom, or anytime I left the room, etc. He kept a yellow legal pad with him and made notes on all of my activities throughout the day. Talk about bullshit!

In late 1996, I donated a kidney to a close friend of mine. I was told, as part of my recovery, to drink as much water as possible to keep my only existing kidney healthy. The bathroom was located directly out my office door and maybe four steps across the hall. I went to the bathroom several times daily, from drinking so much water. Being a radio DJ, I understood the art of the quickest piss possible. I didn't waste my time at the TV station either. I went and got back in record time each time. This didn't stop my supervisor from noting it on the legal tablet. Catching him in the act several times was enough for me to finally speak up about it. I looked over the wall that separated our desks and asked him, "So, do you really enjoy keeping tabs on my bathroom trips every day?" He was surprised I knew what he was doing, and he said nothing.

I vented all of this to a good friend of mine, who happened to work in the accounting department at the station. She and the other lady in accounting told me I should report this to an ombudsman. Since we worked for ASU, we had that service available to us. So during my lunch break, I called the ombudsman service and made an appointment to come down and speak to someone. This had been going on long enough, and I needed to speak up about it. I was forced into being quiet for way too long, because I desperately needed this job. I was making decent money, especially the overtime pay during pledge drives. I also had medical insurance for both Jeffrey and me. There was no way I could have risked losing this job, but enough was enough!

I shared everything with the ombudsman, and she decided we needed to have a group meeting involving the boss and her minion. I wasn't too happy with this, but what could I do? I did, however, like that I had a person outside of the station who would look at the situation without any bias. She had to play fair and listen to both sides of the story. I understood that. A few days later, we had the meeting. I was surprised at how quiet the other two were when the issues were brought up. I was given the right to speak first after the ombudsman brought up my initial complaint. I noticed that my supervisor had brought in the yellow legal tablet, but midway through my opening statement, he hid it beneath the chair. I wasn't about to let him get away with that crap!

"Dan would write down everything I did every day on a yellow legal pad, including how many times I went to go pee," I said. "I was sure he was going to have that legal pad in here for the meeting and bring it out to justify why he was told to be my babysitter, and yes he sure did. But, did you notice how he hid it beneath the chair as I started talking about it? C'mon Dan, bring that tablet of paper out, so you can go through the list of my daily activities. Let's see how many bad things I've done on a daily basis. Let's see how many times I answered the phone, what my conversations were and how many times you saw me go to the bathroom. Oh, and did you time my trips to bathroom too, like you did my phone calls?" He didn't say a word, and I think I even embarrassed him a little bit by calling him out. The lady asked him if he had anything to say, or wanted to show her the tablet. He just said, "No."

My boss spoke up a few times, but to be honest, I don't remember what she said. They really didn't have a leg to stand on. She then asked them if I completed my daily job duties. The answer was yes. She asked them if I caused any problems with any other employees. The answer was no. She asked them if I created any type of issues in the workplace at all. The answer, again, was no. She then wrote down a few notes. She recommended that Dan no longer be in charge of me, and my boss was to assign someone else as my supervisor. She also told my boss, unless she had a real reason to be concerned about me, she shouldn't be assigning someone to watch me in such a manner. She said if I felt I was being harassed in any such fashion, to consult with her again.

I felt like the battle had been won, but I soon realized the war was far from over. I found out Dan was still going to be watching me, but I wasn't supposed to know about it. Within two weeks after the meeting, he resigned and left the station. Honestly, I wasn't the least bit shocked. He was always out for himself, and he didn't think I would fight back. He had positioned himself to get a raise and promotion, based on his tattling of what I was doing every day. When that didn't work in his favor, he found another place to go. Good riddance, asshole! Too bad the same thing didn't happen to my boss.

The station hired another manager to work by her side. He was a much older man named Tex, and he actually treated me very well. My boss then hired a supervisor for my department, instead of promoting me. She moved our office across the hallway from her, claiming it was part of the whole office makeover. Such bullshit! She redesigned the seating to be an open type, with one of those u-shaped office setups. My computer and work area were now completely open to all prying eyes in the room and from across the hallway. Anyone could hear my conversations and see what I was doing on my computer at all times. To make matters even worse, she decided to combine two departments. She doubled my workload and gave me extra duties that weren't part of my job description. Do you think I got a raise for this? Hell no!

141

I not only handled the data entry and balancing duties, but I was now stuck answering the customer service/membership hotline. You could say I was more than a little pissed off at all of this. Things just kept getting worse, and I felt there was nothing I could do about it. I had to take my lumps, because I needed this damn job. There was no going back to the ombudsman for me, because my bully would have just made things even worse than she had proved to do. At least I had my weekend radio gig to help me blow off some steam.

CHAPTER TWENTY ONE

I didn't bother with serious relationships during this time. I was too busy trying to be a mother, dealing with this crap at the TV station, working my weekend gig at the radio station, doing the TV show on occasion, writing for the hockey website and working for the music publication. I enjoyed the friends with benefits type of relationships, because they allowed me to not have to deal with the daily drama of having a man in my life. I could do whatever I pleased, without someone getting upset that I wasn't there for them all the time. My kid came first, career second and men third. That's just the way it was until someone blew my world apart on September 5th, 1999.

We were at a Phoenix Coyotes pre-season game that day. Jeffrey and I always made funny signs, and we ended up on television all the time. It didn't hurt that I was good friends with the director who managed the TV broadcasts of all the games in the arena. My buddy scored us a few extra tickets for my dad and half-sister to come along with us. Jeffrey and I were having a hard time holding our sign up during the game, so this guy came over and offered to go get us some tape during the intermission to hang it on the wall. He missed part of the second period and had to wait for a stoppage in play before he was able to get us the tape. He hung around with us through the rest of the game. My father made a remark at the end of the day that I was going to end up marrying this guy. Yeah right! Not on your life!

This was the first time my father had actually been right about something. Who would have ever guessed this hockey game would bring someone into our lives that would make such a huge impact in such a short amount of time. He became known as the greatest love of my life: Cliff. Within six months, we were engaged. I'll never forget my son telling me that I better marry this guy, or else. They were as much of an instant fit as Cliff and I were. I couldn't have asked for a better mate in my life.

I quit my weekend gig at the radio station, and we planned to go celebrate at Disneyland as a family. It never happened though, because Cliff's cancer had returned. He had just dealt with testicular cancer right before we had met, and he was under the impression that he was cancer free. You can bet I was more than a little concerned about all of this. How could this be happening to us now? Jeffrey and I had finally found someone who we could both be around and truly enjoyed having in our lives. Why now?

We were planning on a September wedding on the ice, exactly one year to the date that we had met. Since I was the team writer for the Coyotes at the time, I had arranged with them to let us do this on the ice during an intermission. It wasn't meant to be. Cliff almost died in July, so we decided to opt for a wedding in the hospital as soon as possible. We were married in the chapel on July 23, 2000 by the minister who had befriended him in the hospital over their love of hockey. The craziness was far from over, and the next seven months proved to be more than I could have ever imagined.

Things had gotten a little strange at the TV station around this time. I had put up with the boss and her crap for over five years. Can you believe, I finally earned her respect, because I married a sick man? She asked me to come into her office one day in late July. I had no idea what she wanted to see me about. I had kept my nose to the grindstone and did whatever they told me to do. So why was I here? She asked me to sit down and said she wanted to talk to me. She congratulated me on my recent marriage and wished me the best. She then said, if I needed to use my vacation time to take care of him, that would be fine. I was a little stunned, thanked her and left the room. What the hell just happened here?

My co-worker, Helene, was concerned that something bad had just taken place, so she came up to me and asked what the boss wanted. I shared what she had said to me, which surprised her as well. I found out, the boss had been forced to give up her job in Detroit as a museum curator to move to Arizona and take care of her sick mother. Okay, so did I just melt the ice queen a little bit here? I took it for what it was. I didn't trust her, and I sure as hell wasn't about to let my guard down, no matter what. I was right in doing so, because she later gave me grief for taking time off to spend with Cliff while he was undergoing his chemo treatments. I knew it was too good to be true.

Since I couldn't take any more time off, I had to find a way to make it all work. My weekly routine consisted of getting Jeff ready and off to school in the morning, going to work at the TV station all day, coming to the hospital after work and having dinner with Jeff and Cliff, taking Jeff home in the evening and coming back up to the hospital to spend the night with Cliff and help the nurses in any way I could. I didn't have a weekend radio gig anymore, so that helped. You could say life was just a bit crazy back then.

In early 2001, I decided I had enough of the crap going on at the TV station. It was time to exit and find a better place to work. No matter how much I loved working with several of my co-workers, the boss and her watchdog had put a real sour taste in my mouth. I had to get away from all of the negativity. I was hired by Verizon as a supervisor, to train people in customer service and data entry. My job was to begin in a few weeks, so I typed up my letter of resignation the morning of February 7th. I placed copies of the letter on the desks of my two bosses and my supervisor. We had a meeting that morning, so no one would receive my letter until after it was over.

I felt really good about my decision, and I went into the meeting with my head held high. Helene and I were talking about my pending departure just as the meeting started. Halfway through the meeting, I was presented with an award from Tex. You could say I was bit more than shocked at this. I had no idea I would be recognized for something I created and on this day of all days! That didn't change my mind though. I knew I needed to get out of there and save whatever sanity I did have.

I had no choice but to part ways with the station, because it was very unhealthy for me to continue working there. I've always been a very healthy person, but the daily stress of the hell I had to endure at work, and all of the other stuff, was just too much. I remember the day I came to that decision. Out of nowhere, I had such an excruciating pain in my shoulder blades that reduced me to tears. It felt like someone had just inserted a blazing hot poker into my body and then laid a ton of bricks on top of me. What the hell was going on now? I didn't need this along with everything else.

I called Cliff, and he told me I should go to the Urgent Care on the way home from work. I stopped in to the clinic before heading to the hospital. The news wasn't as bad as it could have been, but it was bad enough. They said I had shingles. Okay, so what the hell are shingles? I had never heard of shingles, other than the kind you put on your roof. The doctor explained that it was the nerve pain associated with shingles, or as they are commonly known, adult chickenpox. Some people get a breakout, and others don't. I didn't have any bumps on me whatsoever, just this horrific crippling pain in my shoulders. I asked him how I would ever get something like this. He asked me questions about everything going on in my life at the time, and he assessed that I had contracted shingles because of all the stress I had been going through. I'm pretty tough, but damn this shit hurt like hell!

He gave me a prescription for something to get it under control. He also mentioned that, since Cliff was undergoing chemo treatments, it might be best for me to avoid him while I was in the contagious stage. I didn't want to hear this, because he relied on me so heavily at the time. After I left the Urgent Care, I made my way over to the hospital. I talked with his nurse, and she said I could be in the room with him, but I had to wear gloves and a mask over my face. I also had to move my portable cot to the other side of his room at night. I was still allowed to be there, but we had to take precautions. Thank God I could still be there with him and help the nurses.

So here we are, back in the meeting the day I had planned my departure. Helene and I were giggling a little bit, because we both knew what I had planned. Once the meeting was over, we all headed back to our rooms. I heard a gasp coming from my room, and I was sure that it was my supervisor about to go postal as I walked in. She had left the room before I got there and made her way across the hallway to my other boss' office. About 25 minutes later, she came back into our room. She was not very happy about getting my letter of resignation. She told me they had discussed it, and that I was to pack up my personal belongings and return my building key to the campus police that day.

I told her I was planning on fulfilling my two weeks, and that's why I gave my notice now. She wasn't having it. She got nasty with me and told me to get my things together and leave, NOW! Okay, so that was it. I was done, and they weren't even allowing me to finish out my two weeks. She was pissed off at me, because now she didn't have her little grunt to push around, and she was going to have to pick up the slack. I was okay with that. I was finally able to walk out of that building and never look back. It did, however, piss me off that she locked me out of my email account the minute I left the building. What a bitch! Good riddance to this nightmare place!

CHAPTER TWENTY TWO

I was so glad to have this time with Cliff for a few days before the new job was to start. Verizon actually called me, and said they wanted me to start a week earlier than we had planned. I was good with that. I needed to get back to work and make a paycheck, since I was the only one working. Cliff had to sell his truck, because he needed to come up with his share of the rent. He couldn't drive it anymore, thanks to the cancer and his physical limitations. I know it killed him to do that, but what choice did we really have? I couldn't afford to pay the $1000 monthly rent on the house by myself, and it bothered him to have the truck sitting in the driveway and not being able to even get in it.

I went to work at Verizon the following Monday, and it was far from what I was expecting. The job I was hired for was not the job that was given to me. I ended up in a training room with a bunch of other people to become a customer service rep in the phone room, not the supervisor. My pay was only going to be $8.50 an hour and not the $12.50 I was supposed to be getting. What the hell? I couldn't interrupt the class, or speak to anyone, while the morning session was underway. Once we hit the lunch break, I made my way over to the woman who had hired me. I asked her what was going on, since I was under the impression I would be a supervisor and not a CSR. She shrugged me off with the answer that things had changed, and this is what job I now had. You've got to be kidding me!

I left the building and went to call Cliff. He was a bit surprised at my news and asked me why I didn't just leave earlier in the day, instead of sitting through four hours of the training session. He told me I didn't have to stay at the job if I didn't want to. Honestly, I was a bit relieved, but also scared at the same time. I had no idea what I was going to do for a job at this point. I spent the next few days contacting every radio station I could to try and find work. Nothing but a bunch of dead-ends. I went through the newspaper, looking for whatever job I could find in data entry. I beat the pavement for a few days and still had no luck. I was about to go and file for unemployment, when I received a phone call from Cliff's lawyer.

We had an ongoing malpractice lawsuit against his former doctor at the time. The lawyer found out about my situation and said he needed to hire another assistant in his office. He offered me a decent wage, and said I could eventually work up to be a paralegal if I wanted. I was thrilled with this offer, and I accepted.

We had planned for me to start working on a few things, and I made arrangements to come in later that week. He sent me home after our first meeting with a typing program. I had to up my typing speed to his standards if I were to work for him. Okay, challenge accepted. I needed this job desperately, and I've always had a thing for the world of justice anyway. Just when I thought we had something positive to look forward to, it all went to hell again. My life was about to be shaken up in a very unexpected way, that would devastate both my son and me.

I was getting prepared to start the new job with our lawyer the following day, and I was having a rough time sleeping that night. I was awoken several times by Cliff all throughout the night. At this point, we were both sleeping in the living room on the huge sectional we had. He had to lay upright in the recliner, because it was more comfortable for him. I was on the sectional next to him, in case he needed anything. I can remember him complaining that he was hot, so I got the fan and placed it near him to cool him off. He woke me again saying he was thirsty and couldn't quench his thirst enough. The third time he woke me up saying he couldn't go to the bathroom and was having a side pain. He was sweating profusely, and I had no idea what was going on. I was beginning to fear that something was horribly wrong with him.

I asked him if he wanted me to call the paramedics, and he started to argue with me, while almost crying. He didn't know what to do. I tried everything possible to help him, but I was at a loss on what to do next. I was so exhausted, and I remember telling him several times that I would call them if he wanted me to. I told him I was supposed to be starting the new job with the lawyer, and I needed to get my rest. I asked him to make a decision on what he wanted me to do. He couldn't think straight, and was constantly crying that he wasn't sure what to do. I had no choice but to pick up the phone and call the paramedics to come out. They made the decision to load him into an ambulance and take him to the hospital.

My suspicion was right. Something was really wrong with him. I hated that night! It was the last time I ever got to hear his voice, and that hurt like hell. It still does to this day.

I got in my car and followed the ambulance to the hospital. It was still dark out and very eerie. You have no idea what it does to you when you are driving behind an ambulance that is carrying someone you love. The feelings are so overwhelming, and yet you have to stay focused enough to drive. They took him into the emergency area. He was having trouble breathing, and he couldn't really talk.

I explained everything that had been going on prior to us getting there. They gave him something to help calm him down, and they also put him on a breathing machine. This meant they had to insert a tube down his throat. From this point on, he never spoke another word. The cancer had taken over a good portion of his body, and his organs were shutting down. I vaguely remember having the minister there with us at one point. I believe he did, in fact, administer Cliff's last rites. It's all a bit foggy right now.

They eventually moved him to the ICU wing. I had to wait outside while they got everything in place. I can remember being in the waiting room and seeing reports on the television that Dale Earnhardt had just died in a racing accident. I remember several people being out there with me. I didn't want to believe this was the end, and I was trying everything I could to stay positive. There was no amount of prayer or positive thoughts that would help save him now. His body was just too far gone. They had a tube running down into his nose, and all you could see was black stuff coming up through it. This was the cancer from his chest coming out. How do you come back from that?

I stayed the night with him in the ICU. I slept sitting up in the chair right next to his bed. He felt so cold, and all I could do was keep him covered up in warm blankets and hold his hand. I wasn't ready to give up just yet. Sometime during the night, one of his nurses came down to talk to me. We went outside in the hallway, and she brought up the issue of a Do Not Resuscitate form. She asked me if Cliff had one, and I said he didn't. She then explained what would happen if his heart was crashing and what they would have to do to bring him back. What she described was pretty graphic, and since his family is reading this book, I don't want to put it in writing. No one needs to see that.

She then went on to explain that he would continue to be on a ventilator, and the chances of him surviving would be less than 20%, since once they opened him up, the cancer would most likely spread even more. She was very clear with me and never sugar coated anything. I can't tell you how much I appreciated that. I had gotten to know these nurses and nursing assistants very well, with all the time I had spent in the hospital with him. They were so very kind and considerate with me and to Cliff. She went on to discuss what his family and I would have to face, and the decisions we would have to make, in case his heart stopped. I told her I wasn't sure what his family wanted, and I would talk to them about it. I also told her that at one time, he and I were watching a movie about a family faced with this very decision. I could remember what he said so vividly in my mind. "There ain't no way I'm going to ever be a fucking vegetable like that! That is no way to live. Pull the damn plug and let me die!" I at least knew how he felt about it.

I went back into the room and managed to fall asleep while holding his hand. I felt him slipping away from me, and there was nothing I could do except just be there for him. How do you sit beside the love of your life and just slowly watch them die? There are no words to adequately describe that experience, other than feeling helpless, devastated and heartbroken. The next morning I was greeted by his doctor. This wasn't the same asshole who gave him the death sentence. It was a different oncologist on the east side of town we had been seeing for a short time. It turned out that he was also my best friend's doctor, who she had when she was stricken with cancer and died a few years earlier.

He came into the room with tears in his eyes. He apologized to me and said he wished he could have done more. Are you kidding me? You were there for him and did the best you could. You are crying now, and that shows you actually give a damn. I wish his former doctor had actually cared even just a little bit like this man did.

A few hours later, my father came up to the hospital and told me I should go home and get cleaned up. So I bent down to Cliff's ear and whispered, "I'm going home to get a shower and change my clothes. I'll be back in a little while. Don't you dare leave me while

I'm gone." They told me he was in a coma at this point, but I know he heard what I said.

I did a lot of thinking and crying the whole time I was away from him. I knew he was hanging on for some reason, and I believed that reason was me. I knew he loved his family and my son, but I honestly felt like he wasn't letting go, because he was worried about me. He knew everything I had been through before he came into my life. It really bothered him that I had lost a lot of people and had suffered so much hurt and disappointment. I knew what I had to do, no matter how hard it was. I had to be the one to give him permission to let go. I had to be the one to say that it was okay for him to die.

Everything does happen for a reason in our lives. I spent several years going through so much loss in my life, just for this moment in time. My friend David said it so well to me when I questioned why I kept losing so many people. He said, "Their lives and deaths are already predetermined. You were in their lives to learn from their deaths. You are being prepared to deal with something big." He said this shortly before I met Cliff. Who would have eve guessed that this is what the universe had in mind for me during this time? Someone had to be the strong one who could step forward and give him permission to let go. For some reason, I was the chosen one.

I got back to the hospital, leaned down once again, and whispered in his ear. "I'm back, honey. I need to tell you something. I want to thank you for being such a wonderful part of my life. Jeff loves you as his dad, and I am so grateful that he had you in his life. You are, and always will be, the love of my life. Thank you for giving me the love that you did and for making my world a whole lot brighter. I'm going to be okay. I can handle things. I'm a survivor. Jeff and I have each other, and you will always remain the most special part of our lives. If you need to go, it's okay. I'm going to miss you like hell, but I know that you have to do what's best for you. You have my permission to go, baby. I will always love you…always."

CHAPTER TWENTY THREE

A short time later, several of his family members came in. We were all painfully aware of what was going to happen next. We just didn't know how long it would be. His sister and I decided to go up and see the nurses who were working with him in the cancer wing. I bent down, and told Cliff that we would return. Once again, I made sure he understood that he wasn't to leave while I was gone. I know he was in a coma, but I knew damn well he had heard me say it. We had this connection, and he wasn't about to leave me like that. When we returned, his mother mentioned to him that I was back. I reached out my hand and placed it on his leg. At this moment, he opened his eyes, looked around the room at all of us, took a deep breath and then he passed. Just like that, he was gone.

The cries came out, and tears flooded our faces. Something awful, but wonderful, had just happened in that moment. I felt something surge through me from where my hand was placed on his leg, up through my arm and straight through my chest. You might think I'm crazy in saying this, but I believe that his soul or spirit passed through me. I've never felt anything quite like it. Even though we were caught up in the emotion of it all, we noticed he had died with a smile upon his face. He was finally at peace and was no longer suffering. All of us were there with him, and he certainly didn't feel alone. He was surrounded by those who loved him, and that's the way it should be when you leave this earth.

He blew in and out of my life like a hurricane in just 17, short months. It's amazing just how much of an impact he had on both my son and me. It was a real shame that I was finally able to give Jeff a father figure, only for us to lose him like this. We still had each other, and that counted for more than I could have ever hoped for. This time with Cliff was not only a blessing, but it also allowed yet another set of bullies to enter my life: his father, stepmother and his father's sister. Cliff's parents had been divorced for quite some time, and both had remarried other people. I had come to know both sides of the family, and I can honestly say I had a much easier time around Cliff's mom and that side of the family over his dad's.

At first, things were fine, but over time, I felt as if I were being attacked quite often by his dad and that side of the family. The first time I met his stepmother, she made it a point to let me know how she had rescued Cliff when he went through his first bout of cancer. She had taken care of him after he had his surgery, and she went out of her way to make sure he recovered. She expressed how much it meant to her that he relied on her during this time, and they developed a very close bond. Okay, I was fine with this, because family helps out family during times of crisis. Well, it turns out that there was more to this than I even knew. She had fallen in love with Cliff during that time. Yes, his father's wife had fallen for her step-son.

Cliff had his suspicions at one time, but he never did anything with her, because she was his father's wife. He said, even if she wasn't married to his father, he wouldn't mess with her anyway, because she was a disgusting drunk. I didn't know any of this until the week before he died. She had sent a valentine card to our house, and she signed it, "Love, your secret admirer, PE." We were newlyweds at the time. It was a special holiday for us, and he was battling for his life. What the hell was the matter with her? He then shared with me that she had come on to him a while back, but he told her to get the fuck away from him, and that was that.

This wasn't even the worst of it all. In October, Cliff came close to dying a second time. We decided that it was time for him to draft a will. What 35-year-old wants to write his will? No one, but it had to be done, so that we all knew what to do in case something happened. I sat with him one night and made notes regarding what he wanted done with his body, burial or cremation, and what he was going to leave to each person. I typed it up at work the next day, and then we had a notary meet us at the hospital to make it official.

His dad gave me so much grief when he found out about the will. He pulled me outside of Cliff's room and said, "What, are you afraid that I'm going to go to your house and take everything?" What an asshole! Seriously dude? I'm trying to make the best out of a bad situation, so we don't have any issues if something does happen and Cliff dies. We already had two close calls, and we needed to be prepared. I loved him enough to make sure that his final wishes were going to be carried out. No fighting and no bullshit...PERIOD!

There was another issue around the same time that surfaced. He wasn't eating at all, and the doctor discussed possibly having to put a feeding tube in his stomach to help get him some nourishment. I didn't want this to happen, so I did what I could to get him to eat. I would sit there and feed him applesauce, pudding, or anything I could, just to get something into him. His father's sister came up with her husband at the time, and she gave me hell about the feeding tube thing. She didn't pay attention to the fact that I was hand feeding him like I would a baby in order to get his strength back. I had no intention of letting them insert a feeding tube into him if I could avoid it. She reported back to his father, that I was going to let them put a feeding tube in him, and that I was trying to kill him. You have got to be fucking kidding me!

There were so many little things that caused his side of the family to go off on me, for no reason what-so-ever. I was there seven days a week and every free moment of the day, along with sleeping there. I did whatever I could to save this man, and it was never good enough for them. Cliff even asked me to not let them know he was in the hospital one time, because he didn't want them coming around. What does that tell you?

To make matters even worse, his father tried to take his body from the morgue after he died. He was so angry that he wasn't there when Cliff passed away. Not my problem. I called and left a message, and so did others. He didn't come up to the hospital in time. Then I found out later, that he tried to get the body, claiming that Cliff wanted to be buried in Glendale near them. That is not what Cliff wanted at all! He told me, and it was even in his will, that he wished to be cremated and to have his ashes split up among myself and his family. If he wanted to be buried, he would have said so. I'll be damned if I was going to let him destroy his son's last wishes.

In his will, Cliff left his entire Budweiser memorabilia collection to his father. It was very fitting, since the only real time they got along was when they were drinking. I boxed up every last piece of that collection I could find and brought it to the memorial service. I wanted to make sure I never had to deal with that asshole ever again!

As you know by now, my life was never that simple or easy. You would think Cliff's illness and death would have made an impact on those people, but to be honest, all it did was bring out the worst in them. They never thanked me for anything, and I found out they were more than pissed off at me for not letting them get involved in the planning of his service. I tried to reach out to them, but was shut down. It was their way or nothing. Well screw you!

Cliff deserved a lot better than that. I can't even believe his father got upset about some damn stool I supposedly did not include in his batch of goodies from his son. What the hell was he talking about? He said there was some old antique stool worth money that I was keeping from him. Go to hell, you asshole! I had no idea what he was referring to, and I sure as hell wasn't thinking about that crap at a time like this. We parted ways with his side of the family that day, and I had no problem with that at all.

As I've said before, I am no stranger to death, but this one hit me worse than I ever thought anything could. I was not prepared for this at all. Yes, I was strong enough to deal with things, because I had to, but my heart was aching so badly. I felt as if my life was falling apart once again. I couldn't spend the night in our house on the day he died. Jeff and I went home and packed up some stuff, got the bird and headed over to my folks. I couldn't be in that house, knowing he was never coming home to us.

I went back during the daytime and started packing up everything. My lease was about to expire. I hadn't even really started the new job, and I couldn't afford to pay $1000 a month. Besides that, this was our house with Cliff, and with him not being there, it wasn't the same. His mom's side of the family came over and helped me with everything. I was able to pack a lot of his stuff up to give to his family, which helped me in the healing process. I didn't have to come home to all of his belongings staring me in the face day after day.

It wasn't easy moving back home either, but what choice did I have? I had to grieve and heal. I was unemployed and felt like I had just lost my purpose in life. I knew deep down inside that I still had purpose, my son, but at this time, I was simply lost and heartbroken. I still had the lawsuit to deal with too. I made a promise to Cliff that I would not let it go. He wanted to make sure the doctor would have a black mark on his record for not doing what he was supposed to do: provide the proper care. The lawsuit was no longer malpractice and was re-classified as wrongful death.

I found out so many things that angered me, including the doctor's statement in his deposition. He was so cruel and callous. He said he saw thousands of new patients every year, along with thousands of his regular patients. He didn't have the time to look at some blood test that came back from the lab. He only did this if the patient had an appointment to come in. Are you fucking kidding me? You scheduled the blood test. You should have looked at it when it came back, scheduled him to come in, and shared the results. I learned that the tumor markers had quadrupled in this blood test. They could have saved his life had they done the proper follow-up.

Just another damn monkey wrench in the life I was living. No matter how I felt, there was nothing I could do now, except follow through on the lawsuit. You have no idea just how much I wanted to reach out and strangle the doctor when I saw him. It took every ounce of restraint that I had not to. I did, however, stare him down, and made sure he wasn't going to get away with stealing something so precious from our lives. After all the bullshit, we decided to settle out of court. We got the black mark on the doctor's record, but what the hell does that mean anyway? People still went to see this asshole, and he still had his license to practice oncology.

The worst thing I found out through all of this is that, he told another man he was terminal and to get his affairs in order. He told us, since Lance Armstrong had successfully beaten 21 tumors in his fight with testicular cancer, Cliff certainly could beat seven. So while one family had hope, the other had pain and heartache. It turns out that, the man he gave a death sentence to, had become addicted to morphine, and is still alive today! You already know what happened in our case. How the hell could a doctor do something like this, get away with it and keep practicing medicine?

We settled for the sum of $300,000. The lawyers took their share, and by the time all was said and done, we split the rest four ways. Cliff's mom, dad, daughter and I each got $37,000. In all honesty, money was never the issue. We lost someone so precious to us, and nothing could have ever replaced him. Can you believe the doctor didn't even feel any monetary loss at all? You have to be awarded more than a million dollars before a doctor ever sees a penny taken away from him. His malpractice insurance took care of it all.

It's a good thing for him that he was able to keep his luxurious home and cars, not to mention his membership at the local country club golf course. Bastard! I still believe, to this day, that Cliff haunted him. He looked like hell, and a bit disheveled, during the mediation. He died last year, and I was so happy when Cliff's sister told me about it. He got 12 more years than Cliff, and that's not right. He failed his patients and their families. Maybe he became a better doctor afterwards, who knows. Frankly, I'm glad he's gone from this earth.

Can you believe Cliff's father even accused me of killing Cliff? He went so far as to say that I wanted all the money from the lawsuit for myself. What kind of crap is that? I didn't have to give him a damn cent from the lawsuit, but I found it in my heart to do so. He had lost his son, and no matter how much of an ungrateful son of a bitch he was, I wanted to make sure that he got something. My reputation was intact, and I didn't really give a fuck what he said to anyone about me. I knew who I was, and how much I loved Cliff, in spite of it all. I sometimes wish I hadn't made that promise to Cliff to continue on with the lawsuit if he died, but in the end, the doctor had to pay for what he had done to all of us.

CHAPTER TWENTY FOUR

Life went on for us, and I did what I had to do to survive, although my heart ached so badly. I had made the decision to use the money I received in the lawsuit to pay off the Explorer that Cliff and I had bought in 2000. They offered us a death insurance policy to pay off the vehicle in case one of us died. I didn't want to do this at the time, because I felt that it would have told him I believed he was going to die. I also used the money to pay off my student loans and for a down payment on my first house. I decided to have my parents put their house up for sale and move in with Jeff and me once the house was finished.

It took me over a year to get Cliff's estate settled, and he didn't have much at all! I didn't want my mother to have to face this if something were to happen to my father. He had a real bad habit of re-mortgaging their house over and over through the years and had amassed quite a bit of debt. He splurged on lottery tickets, contests and donating money to those cable religious shows for stupid trinkets. He always seemed to find a way to get rid of his money and never be able to pay off his bills.

When they finally sold their house, it was for $119,000. After the bank was paid, and the realtors took their cut, he ended up with about $1,000 in his pocket. They lived in that house for 23 years and he paid $46,000 for it when he bought it. Talk about ridiculous! I never understood why he felt the need to always put himself in so much debt. He wasn't a young guy, for Christ sake!

I had always feared that my mom would end up being on the streets if he died. I would never let this happen of course, but I know she would be in a world of hurt having to pay off what he owed. It's why I made sure to get this all done now while he was still alive. He had all these life insurance policies, but ended up cancelling most of them, except for a very minimal one. He never signed up for the spousal death benefit through his retirement from the government. When he died, it would mean that Mom would never have to worry about money for herself, because she would get a portion of his benefits to live on. He claimed he never spent the money on that benefit, because he was going to outlive Mom. What a bunch of bullshit! It's an argument they still have once in a while all these years later.

I started working at Metro Networks four months after Cliff died. It felt good to get back on my feet and finally have a real job in radio, instead of just a part-time gig or working at some tiny hole-in-the-wall station. I started saving up the additional money I needed for the down payment on the house. It was completed in December of 2002, and we all moved in just before Christmas. It was a bittersweet thing for me. This should have been our family home: Cliff, Jeff and me. Instead, it was his death that gave us this home, and now my family would be sharing it with me. You would think that things would finally level out and life would be a lot easier for me. Nope, there were more speed bumps ahead. Story of my life.

Things started out pretty easy, with no problems at first. I had made an agreement with my dad that he was to pay for the utilities and groceries, because I would be covering the mortgage. This would allow him to pay off all of his other bills. I had never been aware of how much money he was getting every month between his pension, military disability and social security. He acted like he was poor and constantly complained he never had any money. I was a little bit more than shocked to learn that he cleared over $2,600 a month with everything. He was bringing in a hell of a lot more money than I was, and I had to work my ass off for what I did make!

Several of my half-siblings thought he had come into money after he sold his house. One even thought that he owned MY house, and she kept inquiring as to the value of the home. She tried talking us into selling it, because of the current market. Are you serious? I just lived through so much shit, losing my husband, and now I'm trying to make sure that my family, especially my mother, has a home to live in, and you want us to sell it? You're fucking nuts! I kept telling her that it wasn't up to Dad, since I owned it, but she wouldn't listen to me. She was working for some guy at the time that had something to do with selling homes. Frankly, I didn't give a damn what she did, but she had no right to come into my home, ask all about our finances, and what I paid for the house. I was not happy with her at all.

No matter how old you get, living with your parents is not an easy thing to do. I really enjoyed having my mom around. She has always been such a sweet and loving person. I tolerated my dad for the most part. I had to keep reminding myself that I was doing this for my mom. She was way too important to me, and I wasn't about to have her go through any more crap than what she had to. I mainly kept to myself, since I had to work split shifts during the day. Up at 3:00 am and off to work for the 4:30 am to 9:00 am shift. Back again from 2:30 pm to 6:00 pm. I tried napping in-between shifts, but this was never easy, thanks to my natural energy and my dad blaring the volume on the television downstairs. You would think he would have been more considerate, but then again, this is my dad we are talking about.

Don't think that I'm bagging on my dad through all of this. I'm merely stating the facts of how life was for us. I honestly believe, deep down inside, he has a good heart, but for some reason, he always felt the need to control things and the people around him. I ignored a lot of this while growing up, but as I got older, I noticed just how much control he had over my mother. It's sad really, because she never knew how to stand up and fight for herself. She has gotten better at this over the years, but we have to constantly bolster her up and make sure she knows it is okay to have a voice. I think it's one of the biggest reasons why I couldn't find my voice throughout my first relationship and marriage. I really didn't know how to have a voice, because my mother wasn't allowed to have one. We really do pick up things from our parents while growing up, even though we don't think we do.

Eventually, I found my voice, but I went through quite a bit of shit to get to that point. I even had to stand up to my father several times and set him straight. One such occasion came sometime in 2005 when I was involved with someone, my current husband Joe. We had decided that he would move in with me, and of course I discussed this with my folks. They were used to seeing him around all the time, so it was only natural that he would move in. My father and Joe had an agreement that he would pay $50 a month toward the utilities. He would also help me with the mortgage, since he didn't have to pay rent for an apartment anymore.

Over time, my dad would try to play his power trip stuff on Joe. He didn't like him working on stuff in the garage. He was always complaining about the $50, and when was he going to pay it to him. He was told in the beginning that Joe would give him the money on the 10th of every month. It was like clockwork. From the 1st through the 10th, he bugged him constantly for the money. It started to bother Joe, and he shared his feelings with me. I asked my dad to stop with the whole money thing, but of course the "king" of the castle wouldn't quit.

It eventually led us to a knock-down, drag out power trip control fight. I came home from my first shift, and he started arguing with me about why Joe hadn't paid him HIS $50 yet. Once again, I stressed to him about the deal that was made, and how it wasn't the 10th of the month yet. He wasn't having it. He started threatening me, saying that he and Mom would get their own place. You have got to be kidding me, right? After everything I've done to try and help you out, this is the shit you're laying on me right now? I just couldn't believe it! "You won't be able to keep this house if I move out," he said. "Go ahead, get your own place. I'm very capable of paying for this house with or without you," I said back to him as I made my way upstairs. I thought this would be the end of it, but nope, it wasn't.

The next day, he made another remark to me when I came home from my first shift. "I've been looking at mobile homes in a few parks," he said. "I found a nice one that I'm going to buy." My attitude was just okay, whatever. Ask me if I care right now. I'm not playing this damn game with you. I continued upstairs and didn't say another word to him. I knew better than to allow him to engage me in his battle of control. This crap happened several more times over the next two days, and I was really getting tired of it.

Dad said we should just sell the house and go our separate ways. I had a long talk with Joe that night, and he said I should put the house up for sale and call his bluff. If he wasn't serious about all of his threats, then this would shut him up for sure. I wasn't about to go through this shit with Dad all the time. I did all of this out of the goodness of my heart, and he didn't want to do anything except argue with me and try to control everything.

It was heartbreaking for me to consider putting the house up for sale. This was my first real home that I built and owned. I didn't want to have my mom be in the same situation as before, worrying if she would even have a place to live, if he got himself into more debt. My son was in the Air Force at the time, so he basically didn't live there anymore. What was I going to do? I decided to discuss things with my folks that evening. My mom was literally shocked when I brought it up. She had no idea what had been going on. It hurt me so badly to see her in tears because of all this. I think both she and I realized just what kind of man my father was that night.

Calling his bluff didn't even seem to bother him. He was set on finding his own place, no matter what it took. He didn't even care how much this affected my mother. Joe and I found ourselves another house and moved in March of 2006. My folks stayed in the house until April and then moved into a mobile home. My house didn't sell until the end of the summer that year. Once it sold, I went to the bank with my father and paid off the loan on the mobile home. He was hoping to get cash from me, but I wasn't going to allow him to squander the money. I told my mother that she had to make sure to not allow him to re-mortgage the house under any circumstances.

I also paid $1,000 toward the balance on one of his credit cards. I couldn't believe how much debt he still had after having several years to pay things off while he lived in my home. The more things change, the more they stay the same. I shared with my mom just how much credit card debt he had. She decided to speak up about it and demanded that he stop throwing money away on contests and bullshit. She has been able to get him to quit a lot of this stuff, but of course he still wastes money. You can't teach an old dog new tricks. I'm just glad my mom is able to have a clearer vision on all of this where he is concerned. To this day, I keep an eye on things going on with them, because he still complains that he has no money. How in the hell is this possible?

Something happened recently that really upset me, but I was happy to see my mother stand her ground with him. They went on their usual grocery shopping trip, but this time he raised a stink about something so stupid. He told my mother they had to cut back on some of the groceries, and that she really didn't need her canned peaches. She would have her peaches with cottage cheese for a light meal. Now of course, he didn't want to cut back on any of the stuff he normally buys. He couldn't even forego his damn gossip rag in order to save money. Instead, he expected her to give up her canned peaches. What an asshole! I'm sorry but that's just how I feel.

My mother has lived with this kind of stuff for over 50 years. Honestly, I don't know how she does it. As I said before, she does stand up for herself quite a bit more now, but there's no reason why she should have to. He should appreciate that he has such a wonderful, loving woman in his life. When they come over to my house for a visit, I make sure my mother never has to worry about his control crap.

There was a time when the kids and grandkids were here with all of us for dinner and a movie. During the middle of the movie, he announced that they needed to leave, so he could get home to watch his show *Desperate Housewives*. What? Are you fucking kidding me? You want to just up and leave in the middle of the movie for a damn stupid TV show!

I thought I had heard it all. You could tell my mother was really bothered by this. She made it known that she didn't want to go. He didn't seem to care, so I spoke up. "You can go ahead and go home to watch your show. We can take Mom home later after the movie is over." I really don't think he expected that. Both Jeff and Joe echoed what I had said and told him that they would take her home. He then decided to stay, sat back down, and watched the movie until it ended. See, it does pay to stand up to the bully once in a while.

CHAPTER TWENTY FIVE

Bullies come in all shapes and sizes. Many of us have faced bullies at one time or another in our lifetime. Some of us have faced more than our fair share of these types of people than we should have to. Does this mean we have to stay a victim all of our lives and allow this crap to happen? Hell no! It means that we need to pick ourselves up, dust ourselves off and prepare to take control of our life. Even if you aren't being bullied anymore, by staying a victim, you not only allow them to continue the head game of fucking with you, but you never live a fulfilled life. What good is that?

Life has gone on for me, but that doesn't mean I'm not tested from time to time. You would think by now that Mike would leave me alone and not bother with me. For some reason, the court was enforcing the back support he owed me. Keep in mind that I hadn't bothered going back to court over all of this. I basically wrote it off. Jeff was old enough now where it didn't really matter anymore. I had lived without that measly $124 dollars a month all these years, so who really gives a damn. At this point, the back support he owed was somewhere in the $8,000-$9,000 range. I didn't waste the energy to keep up with that shit.

The payments started coming in every once in a while, 90 bucks here, 125 there. Nothing really substantial, but at least it was something. Then there were months at a time where nothing came in. Don't ask me what the hell was going on. I had enough stuff to deal with in my daily life of survival.

Mike has always been the kind of person who liked to sneak back into my life when I least expected it. He had a way of trying to test the level of control that he had over me. I thought he had realized by now, that I no longer feared him, but he had to try once again to get to me. In late 2007, I received a big envelope in the mail. Can you guess who it was from? Yep, the asshole himself, Mike. He sent several legal documents, along with a typed and signed letter. The documents were: Request to Close Child Support Case and Waiver of Paternity Affidavit. You can see these documents and his letter for yourself at the end of the book.

His letter to me was almost a joke, and just made me laugh my ass off when I read it. It was full of his usual threatening attitude and intimidation. Did he really think that, after all this time, I would allow him to victimize me once again? What a dumb ass! Check out the Waiver of Paternity Affidavit. On it he claims we were married at the time of Jeff's conception, yet he had no access to me sexually. Really? We definitely weren't married at the time, dipshit!

Apparently he and his current wife had tried to file bankruptcy, thinking that it would get him out of all the back support he owed for, not just my son, but several of his other children as well. When the bankruptcy didn't release those debts, he sought out to control the situation in the only way he knew how: to scare and intimidate. From what I know, I was not the only one to get this letter from him. Several of the details changed pertaining to each woman and child, but we all got the same thing. I guess he isn't smart enough to realize that his first born son was over the age of 18 now, which meant he would legally have to sue our son for a DNA test, and not me. You've had all these years to go after me for a DNA test, and you do this now? What an idiot!

Sometimes I wish that Jeff wasn't his biological son, but I know for a fact he is. I lived it. I know who I slept with at the time. I know who raped me several months later when I was already pregnant and didn't know it. You can't seriously think that you can threaten me with your DNA test, buddy! Bring it on! He had no legal leg to stand on, and once again I proved to, not only myself, but to him, that his reign of terror against me was over. I totally ignored his letter. I didn't hear anything from him when those 15 days were up. I shared everything with Jeff, since he was old enough. I placed it in the file cabinet, and there it has sat all of these years. No follow through to sue me. Nothing. The threats didn't work, buddy!

Once someone like him realizes that he has no way to get to you, they begin to devise a plan on how to "settle the score" one way or another. It's part of the sociopath mentality. Mike really had no way to do this to me until just recently. It's the main reason why I am telling my story. I never set out to write THIS book. I had other things in mind, but this is the story that has to be told. I guess it's my fault in a way. I opened the door to it happening, and it really pisses me off more than you can imagine.

Not long ago, my daughter wanted help with the family tree. She was newly engaged and wanted to know all about her family heritage. She was making a tree on the ancestry website. She sent me the link, and I began to fill in the blanks for her. I wanted to help her as much as I could, and I didn't think that things would go in the direction they did. I was happy when she connected with her two half-brothers, but not so happy with the connection to Mike.

I have often wondered if I should have shared the whole ugly truth with her years ago when I found her. She has no idea what she is in for when it comes to him. I didn't think she would bother with Mike, but knowing what I do now, there's no doubt that something is developing between them. Let's not forget, he is the one who gave her away, NOT ME! He never wanted girl children. Hell, he never wanted any of his children! I wanted MY child! Once again, he is trying to rip my child away from me, and he has pretty much succeeded for now.

A while back, she asked me not to post anything really personal on her Facebook page, because she didn't want to upset her mother. Not a problem. I get that she really isn't my daughter, and I can't upset her relationship with the only mother she has ever known. She obviously hasn't gotten to know me enough over these past nine years to truly understand the kind of person I am. I'm not sitting around crying every day that I lost her. I got over that gut punch years ago. Life had to go on for me. I would have been a real mess, and not much of a mother to Jeff, if I allowed that one moment in my life to screw me up forever.

I basically backed off and just watched her life from afar. I looked at her posts when they came up in the news feed. I copied a few of her wedding pictures and put them in a folder on my computer. I wanted to have something for myself and to show my folks, since they don't have access to the internet. I never trolled or stalked her page. I am not like that. I frankly don't have the time to be doing that. My life is very full with running a business, and my free time is limited.

It was on her birthday of this year that really changed things for me. I went on her page for the first time in a long time. I posted Happy Birthday Lynsey! That's it. It's what I saw right below my post that upset me. "Happy Birthday, baby girl!" Really? You have got to be fucking kidding me! "Happy Birthday, baby girl!" posted by none other than Mike himself. How is it that I am the only one who gave a damn about this child, and I'm not allowed to post something so personal, yet this asshole, who ripped her away from me, can declare publicly she is his baby girl? I once again felt the rip in my heart, and I couldn't believe what I was seeing. This could not be happening right now, but it was.

Seeing this post on her page felt like a dagger through my heart. I had fought for so long to protect these kids from the ugliness, and here it was staring me dead in the face. I never had to worry about it with my son, because he had lived through some of it. My daughter was basically a stranger to it all. I understand her curiosity in wanting to reach out to her biological father, possibly to fill a void, but the truth is the truth, not his bullshit made up lies! I had no idea what he was telling her at that point. How could I know? She wasn't even sharing things with me anymore. I was beginning to

179

wonder why she was so distant from me. She had even restricted my view to her Facebook page.

That day was really tough for me. I couldn't help but cry. I am human, and this did hurt me, but what could I do? I couldn't write to her and say anything about how much it hurt. I had to take it for what it was: a cheap shot by my ex-abuser to get to me, and he fucking did! I'm sure he knew it. He thrives on this kind of stuff. The next shock was seeing that my son Jeff had friended his father as well! That was when I made the call to my son to express the heartache I had just felt from both of my children. As I explained earlier, he told me why he did what he did. He has always had a good heart, and I understand why he felt the need to help his sister, but in this case, there really is nothing he could do.

So here we are at the moment where I reveal to you the whole reason why I started on this venture of sharing my ugly story. I have always believed that people can change, but in this case, Mike has not changed, and he never will. See for yourself as I share his letter to my son Jeff via Facebook messenger, word for word. Yes I know the grammar is bad, but I will not change it, since these are Mike's words. You will see what I mean about the mind fuck he is trying to do to my son. Can you only imagine what he has said to my daughter? He said he was going to tell the truth, and Jeff may not like it. So much for that.

Conversation started July 25
7/25, 5:32 pm

"Well I will try to keep it short as possible. Your mother and I got together and we dated for awhile. we broke up and about 9 months later she showed up on my door step one night. she was pregnant with you, and then we got back together. She had you then 3 months later we got married. Shortly after almost 1 year later she had a baby girl named Lyndsey and Robin didn't want her parents to know about it, so your uncle bruce and I swore to her that their parents would never find out so we both hid the baby and when she was born Robin gave her up for adoption. shortly after that, I wasn't aloud to touch Robin in any way shape or form. Later we bought a trailer in chandler AZ. and then we were rear ended by a drunk driver and totaled out the car, and hospitalized Robin. We got a settlement from insurance, 15,000 dallors and she blew it in two weeks. She then left you inside a car one day when she went inside some store, then you grabbed the gear shifter and put the car into a store. later another day, I came home and she was in the living room with another guy that I used to work with. It wasn't pretty. I just left, filed for divorce and she told everyone I was the bad guy. I was the one that forced sex on her and after that I lost everything. Years later, your uncle bruce and Robin pulled some strings with her father and had me arrested for not paying child support which was bogus because I had 20,000 dallors in receipts that showed she received the money. But that wasn't enough, she wanted more and further threatened to shoot me and then went before another judge and pressed for child support and had me arrested again and put in prison because she claims I never paid a penny. after I got out, I came home after loosing everything I came home to my parents and family. Now I finnaly got all child support paid off and I am now free and clear of everything. I have been married for 17 years now and just enjoying life."

Now you have just seen it for yourself, in his own words. You've read the story thus far. You've seen that 90% of this letter is bullshit and 10% of it is truth. Okay, now here is what I'm going to do. I am going to break this letter down and show you all where the truth is and where the lies are. It's a real pain in the ass that I have to justify all of his statements about our life together, but it is what it is. So here we go...

"Well I will try to keep it short as possible. Your mother and I got together and we dated for awhile. we broke up and about 9 months later she showed up on my door step one night. she was pregnant with you, and then we got back together. She had you then 3 months later we got married. "

You have all read the history between us. We met when I was 13. He tracked me down by using my CB signal and appeared on my doorstep. We were in several relationships before we ever even made it to the altar. Nowhere does he mention this fact. He says we broke up and nine months later, I showed up on his doorstep. Really, asshole? He seems to forget that I was four-and-a-half months pregnant when I called him. I never came over to see him. Hell, I had to track him down just to tell him. I felt that it was the right thing to do, as I stated earlier in the story.

He doesn't even bother to mention that we broke up again within a few weeks, and that he came looking for me when I was about ready to have the baby. He doesn't mention that he begged me to take him back and marry him. He doesn't mention the fact that I am the one who didn't want to get married right away. He at least had the fact right about being married three months after Jeff was born. Remember the document that stated we were married, and he wasn't having sex with me when Jeff was conceived? His last sentence in this statement proves he even knew that we weren't married when I was pregnant.

"Shortly after almost 1 yr later she had a baby girl named Lyndsey and Robin didn't want her parents to know about it, so your uncle bruce and I swore to her that their parents would never find out so we both hid the baby and when she was born Robin gave her up for adoption."

He told the truth about Lynsey being born, but he lays it all on me about not wanting anyone to know about her. You all know by now the story behind losing my daughter. It was his doing. I wish I would have been stronger, but I wasn't. He took control, and he is the one who gave her away, NOT ME! My parents had no idea. I was pretty sure my brother had no idea either. He never swore to me anything like that back then. Hell, if he had known, he may have been able to put a stop to Mike's plan to get rid of the baby. I called my brother after reading this letter, and he told me that he never knew until I told the whole family. Just as I had thought. It's amazing how Mike's memory says differently and throwing my brother under the bus like that. Wow!

"Shortly after that, I wasn't aloud to touch Robin in any way shape or form."

Really? Not how I remember it at all. I wasn't allowed to say no when he took whatever he wanted, regardless of how I felt. Remember the new pregnancy scare I had? Remember how I talked about him saying that "we would keep this one and raise it as a challenge?" So much for any truth in this statement.

"Later we bought a trailer in chandler AZ. and then we were rear ended by a drunk driver and totaled out the car, and hospitalized Robin. We got a settlement from insurance, 15,000 dallors and she blew it in two weeks."

Again, another bunch of bullshit tied into this partial truth. We were living in the trailer in Chandler before Lynsey was even born. She was conceived there. Yes, we were hit by a drunk driver, but I never went to the hospital. I went home that night. As far as the settlement money goes, I have no recall of the amount as I stated before, but how could I have spent any of it, other than on the medical bills? You all read this part in the story yourself. He was a very controlling man, and there was no way I could have gotten away with spending that kind of money, because he controlled everything in our home.

"She then left you inside a car one day when she went inside some store, then you grabbed the gear shifter and put the car into a store."

Once again, a partial truth. He decides not to share the details of what really happened. I didn't go into a store. You have all read the details of this incident. I went in my workplace to get my paycheck and didn't turn off the engine. I was told to get in, not shut the engine off, get out and get home as quick as I could. Yes, I take responsibility for my part in this, but he should also bear some responsibility as well.

"Later another day, I came home and she was in the living room with another guy that I used to work with. It wasn't pretty. I just left, filed for divorce and she told everyone I was the bad guy. I was the one that forced sex on her and after that I lost everything."

Another fucking lie! I would really like to know who this guy is who I was supposedly fucking in our home when he walked in and caught us. Seriously? How is this even possible? I didn't even know any of his co-workers. I was in a very controlling and abusive relationship. The last thing I would ever do was cheat on him. I wouldn't have known how to do something like that. I was scared to death of him and what he would do to both Jeff and I. The fact that he forced himself on me over and over, made me not even care about having sex at all. Why on earth would I screw someone else when I fucking hated it! And he just up and left after that? Really? You have all read the part where he actually walked out on me that day at my parent's house after my mom stood up and defended me from him trying to get the title to my car in his name. His memory regarding all of this is really fucked up big time! And by the way, he didn't lose a damn thing. He moved on and got married again, as you all have read in this story.

"Years later, your uncle bruce and Robin pulled some strings with her father and had me arrested for not paying child support which was bogus because I had 20,000 dallors in receipts that showed she received the money. But that wasn't enough, she wanted more and further threatened to shoot me and then went before another judge and pressed for child support and had me arrested again and put in prison because she claims I never paid a penny."

Wow, really? Lies, lies and more lies. My brother and I never did any of this. Our father never did a damn thing like this. We could never count on my father for anything like this at all. Twenty Thousand

Dollars? He never owed me this much as far as I know of. I've always believed that he owed me in the area of $8,000-$9,000, and I have never said anything otherwise. Receipts for paying me $20,000? Hmmm. I have all the DES and child support printouts that show what he has been paying me. This is the official record, and there is no way he could have anything showing he paid me that kind of money. I'd like to see those receipts. I didn't want more. I stopped worrying about it and just worked my ass off to raise my kid by myself.

Threatened to shoot him? Wow! That never happened during this time, unless he is referring to the day where he drew my blood and struck the final blow that caused me to fight back, which eventually led to him walking out on me. Remember this part of the story? That's when he was sitting in the recliner and I grabbed him by the back of the hairline and pulled him off of the chair. I drug him over to the wall where those rifles were. I slammed his head up against the wall at least a half a dozen times. Remember my words: "How does it feel, you son of a bitch? How do you fucking like it? How does it feel, mother fucker?" I still don't recall any threats of using a gun on him. Failing memory again there, buddy?

Went before another judge and had him arrested and put in prison? Wow! Where was I when this happened? I didn't have that much pull in the legal system, and I sure as hell didn't have the time to go after this asshole over and over again. In fact, it was revealed to me recently that this didn't involve me at all. It was referring to his second wife, but yet in his mind, he is seeing this as all me. It was her and her father that did this, not me. He owes her the $20,000, not me. It's amazing how he can mix up two of his wives and make them into one person. That is so fucked up! She even told me she always had a feeling that he pursued her for a relationship because we looked similar.

"After I got out, I came home after loosing everything I came home to my parents and family. Now I finnaly got all child support paid off and I am now free and clear of everything. I have been married for 17 years now and just enjoying life."

Who knows what the hell happened when he got out. He wasn't in my life. So what if he moved back home. Good for him. The BIG LIE in this sentence is: "Now I finnaly got all child support paid off and I am now free and clear of everything."

Bullshit, bullshit, bullshit!!!! I am still getting child support payments today! I can prove this very easily. I have a savings account set up, into which the payments are automatically deposited. Before my grandkids were born, I was using this money to fund my film projects. Now that the grandkids are here, the money is set aside for them and their future. You can see a snapshot of my bank account at the end of the book, which will show those deposits. It will show the payments that have come in for the past year. You can also see the official documents from DES proving that he is still on the hook and paying me back support or "Arrears."

So, he is all paid up and doesn't owe anything, huh. That's what he wrote in July. Look at the latest payment that just came in! Gotcha, mother fucker! Another HUGE LIE! You are most definitely not free and clear of your child support debt. You are definitely not all paid up. I know for a fact that you still owe support to others as well. Fucking liar!!!!

The whole truth, the ugly truth, is now there for everyone to see. No more bullshit, no more lies. If we all look at his version of the story, it's a very small and condensed version. I was just a blip on his radar of life, but yet 30 years later, he continues to plague my life in the only way he knows how. He is poison. His words are vicious and unforgiving. He has always left wreckage in his path. He never was the victim, but yet claims that we have all victimized him.

He may have been a victim of his own childhood, but that didn't give him the right to make me, my children, his many other children and his other spouses victims as well. He had a responsibility to rise above his own shit and make a better life for himself and others who he claimed to care about. If he had become a better person, I would have gladly accepted a relationship between him and my children. Knowing that he hasn't changed at all just sickens me inside. How can someone spew so much garbage and not even feel any responsibility or remorse for his actions?

One could only hope that my daughter will see this story and realize the truth before it's too late. I honestly don't think this will happen. She has already made it a point to tell my son that she doesn't want to hear about any drama, because she has enough of her own to deal with. She says that she has heard so many things, that she doesn't know what to believe. Really? Wouldn't you want to know the REAL truth behind why you were given up for adoption? I did tell her some things, but I didn't share everything, like all the shit I had to endure during that time. I sometimes wish I had. That is probably the biggest regret I have, other than not being able to stand up to Mike and save my child. I wish I could save her now, but I have to just let it be. She is old enough to make up her own mind. It's not up to me anymore to protect her. She doesn't want to hear the truth. That is the real shame in all of this.

I tried to contact her by phone after this letter came to light. She didn't answer my call. I decided to call back and leave a message for her to call Jeff and me. She didn't bother. She instead sent Jeff a message, and that's when she stated she didn't want to hear about the drama. It's not fucking drama, damn it! It's the truth! Why can't she understand that we are just trying to protect her from his wrath? I have the proof, not him.

At this point in my life, I have no other choice but to let it go. It's up to her to come to me now. I will no longer try to reach out and make the effort to get her out here to meet all of us. It's out of my hands from this point on. My last communication with her was this message I sent to her in July.

"I spoke to Jeff this morning, and he shared your message with me. I can see that you have a tremendous amount of things going on in your life. The last thing I would ever do is inundate you with anything else. Just know that you have family here, and that you are loved. You were always wanted, and if I had been strong enough back then, you would have been with Jeff and me no matter what. I may not have been your mother, but in my heart you will always be my child. If you ever need anything, or just want to talk, you can always call on me or your big brother. We are here for you, no questions asked and nothing ever expected in return."

CHAPTER TWENTY SIX

When I started this book, it was not only to tell the whole gut wrenching truth, but to help my daughter understand what really happened in my life that led to her being put up for adoption. It has definitely taken on a much bigger meaning than I ever thought it would. So many of us go through our lifetime experiencing things that can definitely destroy us. We live in silence for so long. This is no way to live. We have to find a way to rise above it all and have a voice. That's what this book is for me in so many ways. I have found my voice. I have also given a voice to those who have not been able to find theirs as of yet. They still suffer in the shadows, but not so silent anymore. They have reached out to let me know how important it is for me to continue with what I am doing.

Many people have known my story over the years, but being the private person I am, I managed to keep some of the shit quiet. This has definitely changed now. There are many other things that have happened in my life, which also freaked me out, but I managed to get through them in the best way I knew how. By living through my first hell of a marriage, I was able to spot something in my second that helped me make the decision to end it. I shouldn't have listened to my father's advice to stick it out another week, but that's all in the past now. By surviving those two marriages and making it out alive, I developed a whole different attitude toward things. I had to assume I would always be a target, if I didn't go into things with my eyes wide open. I know this sounds extreme, but to be honest, that's the way it had to be. I had to protect the one child I was entrusted to raise.

Everyone knows that we tend to attract the same type of people into our lives. Proof came for me in the first two men I had been married to. They were similar in looks, and they both had some real issues to deal with. They came into my life and taught me a few things that I never thought I should have had to learn, but this was my destiny, my fate. I was there for a reason. I thought it was love at the time, but what the hell did I know? I was really too young to understand it all. I get it now. It cost me a hell of a lot, but in the end, I am a much stronger person for having gone through it all.

I almost feel as if I'm bulletproof at times. Yes, I can still feel things, and still hurt, but the difference now is, I know I can survive anything that comes my way. Mike was, and still is, so self-centered. He can't even see past his own lies and admit the truth of what has happened. Hell, maybe he is so fucked in the head that he honestly believes his lies are the truth. I understand that is a trait of a sociopath. They create their own little worlds, and the only person who matters is themselves. Everyone is out to get them, so they go to extreme lengths to protect themselves. Honestly, I wouldn't want to live like that. It's a waste of the life we have been given.

I remember a line from a movie called *"Like the Spider"* that was made by my friend Randy Huckabone. "Every living thing deserves a chance. A chance to be better. A chance to make a difference. And when they chance themselves out…In the end, everything dies. It's a matter of how they get there that defines them." I am at peace with who I am, and what I have lived through. I wonder if Mike can say the same thing? I wonder if he can even comprehend the damage that he has caused over the years?

He claims he lost everything. Well, buddy, let me tell you that you don't know anything about real loss until you lose something you love more than yourself. I seriously doubt he even knows what real love is. I didn't know until I met Cliff, and I went through two marriages and several relationships before I even got to that point! Love is kind, but can also cause pain. Real love is not what I had with Mike. If it were, he would have never used my children against me. He would have never threatened to kill my son in front of me, or threatened to kill me. He would have never abused me in the fashion that he did. He would have never given away our daughter. He would have never treated his other children or spouses so badly. He would have been an important part of his children's lives from day one.

Shit happens between us adults, and relationships sometimes don't last, but what we have to remember is that the children need us. They are the most important thing in our lives. We have to learn to set aside any bad feelings we have for one another and be there as a united front for the children. Too bad Mike didn't give a damn about any of his kids, and he chose to leave them in the dust while he continued on living his life. He can't blame his father for that, it's all on him.

No matter what your situation is, there is someone who has gone through something very similar. I have always known that I am not the only person who has gone through crap like this, but I had no idea just how widespread this problem is. There weren't a lot of resources for me out there back then. There are many places that offer help now. I know it's a scary thing to ask for help, but seriously, if I take one thing from my own experience, it's that we need to get ourselves to a healthier and much safer place. If not for us, then we have to do it for our children. We are strong. We must believe that.

I never realized just how strong I was, but I have learned that over time. We can't allow the bullies to win. We can't allow those who control us to take over our lives and make us wish more for death than to be alive. Yes, I went through a time like this, but I am glad to say that I am still here, and I did not give up.

Even when you think you are alone, you do have a voice. Even if you feel that no one is there to help you, use your voice to reach out. There are many of us survivors out here in the world, and we can help you. You can lean on us to get you through this. I can truly understand and relate to the pain you have been going through. I'm not in your head, nor do I know what's in your heart, but I can honestly say I've been there and back. You've seen this in my story. I'll be damned if I will let Mike continue to make me his victim! I will never say that I know how you feel, but I will be there to help give you a voice. I will help you regain the strength you need to carry on and get through this. We are all on this earth to learn and to help one another.

If you're a person who is struggling with your own demons, then please get some help. Reach out: there are people who can help you. Don't let your past define your future. Anyone can change, if they really want to. It's never too late to change and make a better life for yourself. There is no reason for you to continue to hurt others and yourself. You are human. We all feel and experience things in life. I know it's not easy for you to ask for help, and you may not even realize you need it. You do have a choice to make things better for yourself. I know that life may not have been easy for you so far, but trust me, things will get better. You don't have to remain a victim. You have to let go of all the negativity and find your little piece of happiness. It's there if you really want it.

Most importantly, to anyone who sees a friend, a family member, a child, a spouse or anyone around you struggling, reach out to them. Give them your support, and help however you can. Sometimes a kind word is all they need to get back on the right track to a much healthier and happier life. It's the one thing that I wish I had back then, but I felt I had nowhere to go, and no one would listen. I suffered in silence for so long, and I shouldn't have had to. I shouldn't have had to live with a man who said he loved me in one breath and threatened to kill me or my child in another. I shouldn't have had to lose my child at the hands of her father. No one should have to live like that.

It's up to all of us to make the change happen. We are all ultimately responsible for breaking the cycle. I'm certainly glad I did. I have an awesome son who is now a father to his own two little ones. He has also formed wonderful relationships with his two half-brothers from Mike's second marriage. Sue and I have even grown closer over the years. Good things can happen out of tragedy. We just have to find the inner strength to rise above it all and move on with our lives in the best way that we can. Above all we need to remember that we are no longer victims. We are SURVIVORS!

Symbol of spiritual growth and transcendence.
In the tradition of the Lakota Sioux, it is the symbol for change,
freedom and the courage needed to achieve these goals.

Victim No More! is a must read for anyone who has been a victim of domestic abuse, or who knows someone who they believe is suffering under its tyranny now.

The signs mapped out by author Robin Coté are there for all to see and read. Heed them. Help Robin to wipe out domestic abuse, and take as your mantra, Victim no more!

Author Debra Shiveley Welch

Sinni, the Warrior Goddess

Like the Phoenix, she rises from the burning rubble

and soars high above the mountaintop.

The sun's rays penetrate the dark clouds,

sending beams of radiating light through her

golden hair. A lightining bolt shaped

staph in one hand and ashes of days gone by

in the other. She rides the wind, releasing

the ashes into oblivion. She is free.

Robin Y. Cotè

If you need help to get out of a bad situation, please contact:

The National Domestic Violence Hotline
1-800-799-SAFE (7233)
thehotline.org

National Suicide Prevention Lifeline
1-800-273-8255
suicidepreventionlifeline.org

Rape, Abuse, and Incest National Network
800-656-HOPE (4673)
rainn.org

Bullying Hotline
1-866-210-3388
stopbullying.gov

There are many organizations locally or on the internet you can contact as well. Don't suffer in silence. You are not alone.

BIRTH HOPE ADOPTION AGENCY, INC.

AGREEMENT

Michael ███████ and BIRTH HOPE ADOPTION AGENCY, INC. (BIRTH HOPE)
acknowledge that Robin ███████ is pregnant with child and in need of
financial assistance, food, utilities, phone .
Michael ███████ hereby requests that BIRTH HOPE pay for Financial
Assistance, food, utilities, phone .
for Robin ███████ and her child in Phoenix .

Michael ███████ agrees that if BIRTH HOPE makes such payment(s) that
He , Michael ███████ , will repay BIRTH HOPE at the offices
of BIRTH HOPE at 3225 North Central Avenue, Suite 1010, Phoenix, Arizona 85012,
within thirty days of the date on which Robin ███████ delivers her child,
all monies advanced or paid by BIRTH HOPE for the benefit or for the account of
Robin ███████ and her child for financial assistance, food,
utilities, phone .
Michael ███████ and BIRTH HOPE acknowledge that Robin ███████
is under no obligation to place her child for adoption with any adoption agency
in any of the United States, including BIRTH HOPE; and, they acknowledge that
Robin ███████ may keep her child or may place her child for
adoption, as she alone chooses.

Michael ███████ and BIRTH HOPE hereby agree, nothing herein contained
to the contrary withstanding, that if Robin ███████ , of her
own volition places her child with BIRTH HOPE for purposes of adoption, in
Arizona, then, and in that event, all obligations incurred by Michael
███████ by this document are released, waived and discharged.

michael ███████   June 18, 1986
Signature   Date

███████   ███████
Social Security Number   Name of Employer

███████   ███████
Resident Address   Address

Chandler   AZ 85224   Mesa   AZ
City   State Zip Code City   State Zip Code

███████   ███████
Area Code   Telephone Number Area Code   Telephone Number

Accepted, in Phoenix, Arizona
BIRTH HOPE ADOPTION AGENCY, INC.

Lou ███████   June 18, 1986
Representative   Date

I, Michael ██████████, Social Security No. ██████████, being
the father of Jeffrey ██████████, born on July 19, 1985 in
Mesa, Arizona, do hereby relinquish and give up all my rights to
the care, custody, control and visitation of the minor child
Jeffrey ██████████ to his mother, Robin ██████████.
I hereby acknowledge that I will no longer be responsible for
any support to the minor child due to the fact that I relinquish
all my rights and any claim to the minor child, Jeffrey ██████████
██████. I will no longer be declared as the father to the minor
child.

mıchael ██████████
Signature

SUBSCRIBED AND SWORN to before me this ___23___ day of _March_
19 _90_ by ██████████ _Michael_

MY COMMISSION EXPIRES _My Commission Expires Aug. 31, 1993_   _Michael Dennell_
Notary Public

This is to inform you that I am pursuing legal action to obtain DNA testing on:
Jeffrey ███████████████
What this means to you is that once it is established that I am NOT the biological parent of your kid, then you will be REQUIRED to repay ALL the child support I have paid PLUS interest. Then I will sue you in court for the emotional trauma that you have caused me for the past 20 years.

You and I already both know that I am not the kid's father. Now you can do this the easy way or the hard way. The easy way being that you can sign the enclosed **REQUEST TO CLOSE THE CHILD SUPPORT CASE** in front of a notary, send me a copy and send the original to DCSE in the enclosed postage paid envelopes. Or you can do it the hard way and we can drag this through court. Imagine how your kid is going to feel about you when he finds out that you have lied to him all these years and I do have proof that you have lied all these years.

You have 15 days from the date this is mailed to submit the completed document to DCSE and a copy to me or I will pursue legal action to obtain the DNA testing.

Michael ████████

PS. You will also be responsible for my court costs when the DNA tests show that I am not the kid's father.

REQUEST TO CLOSE CHILD SUPPORT CASE

NAME: _____

ATLAS CASE NUMBER: _____

I want to close my case with the Division of Child Support Enforcement (DCSE). I understand if I want child support services in the future, I must reapply with DCSE. I understand that by closing my case with DCSE, credit reporting, asset seizure, automatic income withholding, tax and lottery intercepts cannot be done and locate services will only be provided though a separate application process and payment of a fee.

I understand that unless I complete a new application for child support services, no more action will be taken on my case by DCSE unless the child(ren) of this case receive TANF benefits. DCSE has the right to seek any unpaid TANF that has been paid for the support of my child(ren).

_____   _____
Your Signature   *Date*

STATE OF _____   )
)   ss.
COUNTY OF _____   )

Subscribed and sworn or affirmed and acknowledged before me this date,_____

Notary Public_____

My Commission Expires:_____

FCSE0001 F0134 (07-07)W

ARIZONA DEPARTMENT OF ECONOMIC SECURITY
Division of Child Support Enforcement

WAIVER OF PATERNITY AFFIDAVIT
(THIS IS A LEGAL DOCUMENT, PLEASE TYPE OR PRINT IN BLACK INK.)

AFFIDAVIT OF PRESUMED FATHER

STATE OF ██████████)
)   ss   *AFFIDAVIT*

County of   St. Joseph   )

I,   Michael ██████████ , being duly sworn upon my oath, depose and say
     (Presumed Fa... ...le, Last)

that I am the former/~~present~~ husband of   Robin ██████████ and that at the time of conception of
                                               (Name of Child's Mother - First, Middle, Last)

     Jeffrey ██████████
                 Child 1 Name (First, Middle, Last)

                 Child 2 Name (First, Middle, Last)

                 Child 3 Name (First, Middle, Last)

I was married to   Robin ██████████ but did not have sexual access to her during the conception period(s)
                 (Name of Child's Mother - First, Middle, Last)

Therefore, I am not the natural father of the above-named child(ren) and hereby relinquish and waive all legal rights that I might have to the above-named child(ren).

Further, I do not object to any proceeding to establish paternity against the natural father. I waive my right to notice of and my right to appear at any hearing for the above-named child(ren).

Dated: **November 5, 2007**

Signature: *[signature]* ██████████

Subscribed and sworn or affirmed and acknowledged before me this date: *NOVEMBER 2, 2007*

My Commission Expires: *JAN 08*   Notary Public *Barbara M Hart*

Account Activity

Personal Accounts

ROBIN XXXX

Activity Summary

Current Posted Balance	
Pending Withdrawals/ Debits	
Pending Deposits/ Credits	
Available Balance	

Transactions

Find Transactions
Description or Keyword   **AZ CHILD SUPPORT DES IVD D0**
Dates5   **Last 12 Months**
Amounts or Check Numbers
Type

Date ↓	Description	Deposits / Credits	Withdrawals / Debits
Pending Transactions			
11/19/14	AZ CHILD SUPPORT DES IVD D007915909	$267.68	
Posted Transactions			
10/20/14	AZ CHILD SUPPORT DES IVD D007859091 ROBIN COTE	$149.91	
09/16/14	AZ CHILD SUPPORT DES IVD D007797914 ROBIN COTE	$149.90	
08/25/14	AZ CHILD SUPPORT DES IVD D007754357 ROBIN COTE	$27.68	
07/18/14	AZ CHILD SUPPORT DES IVD D007688774 ROBIN COTE	$394.36	
06/13/14	AZ CHILD SUPPORT DES IVD D007622223 ROBIN COTE	$149.91	
05/19/14	AZ CHILD SUPPORT DES IVD D007570285 ROBIN COTE	$272.13	
04/17/14	AZ CHILD SUPPORT DES IVD D007510054 ROBIN COTE	$272.13	
03/21/14	AZ CHILD SUPPORT DES IVD D007456232 ROBIN COTE	$27.68	
02/18/14	AZ CHILD SUPPORT DES IVD D007390265 ROBIN COTE	$103.28	
01/24/14	AZ CHILD SUPPORT DES IVD D007343730 ROBIN COTE	$318.76	
12/16/13	AZ CHILD SUPPORT DES IVD D007270121 ROBIN COTE	$149.91	
Totals		**$2,283.33**	**$0.00**

QTCPNC ████████████   Date: 10/07/14   NOC1 (02/13)
Division of Child Support Enforcement
P.O. Box 40458
Phoenix, Arizona 85067

RE: ████████████
                                    ████████ M

ROBIN ████████
████████

DEPARTMENT OF ECONOMIC SECURITY
Your Partner For A Stronger Arizona

Janice K. Brewer   Clarence H. Carter
Governor   Director

En Espanol al lado reverso
El tiempo de esta informacion es delicado

NOTICE OF COLLECTIONS

This notice tells you how the Division of Child Support Enforcement (DCSE) distributed and disbursed support payments for your case(s) in the month listed. DCSE must follow state and federal laws and court orders to disburse support payments. The amount shown in current support may include spousal maintenance if it was ordered in the same order with child support and was collected by DCSE. The amount shown in arrears may include payments made on interest and/or spousal maintenance arrears. If you have any questions about your case, or about this notice, you may contact your local child support office. If you disagree with the amounts listed in this notice, you may request an administrative review. See the information page about requesting an administrative review. This notice only includes payments made to the Arizona DES Division of Child Support Enforcement and processed as of the date of this notice.

If your address or telephone number changes, you must notify us immediately.

Payments received and distributed/disbursed in September , as well as payments previously received and identified for release to your case(s) in September are listed on the following pages:

208

Information About Assigned Arrears

While you are receiving cash assistance, any child support that is received will be kept by the state to repay the cash assistance paid to you in accordance with federal law. The child support you assign to the state is limited to the amount of cash assistance benefit paid to your family. The state may not keep more support money than the total amount given to you in cash assistance.

When you are no longer receiving cash assistance you will receive your current support. Unpaid support for the months after you stopped receiving cash assistance is owed to you. You will receive that unpaid support until those amounts are paid in full. After you are paid, any amount assigned to the state will be applied to the state debt for the cash assistance you received. There is an exception in that amounts received from federal tax offsets apply to the state debt before they are applied to support owed to the family.

If you disagree with the distribution or disbursement of support payments as listed in this notice, you may file a written request for an administrative review pursuant to A.R.S. § 46-408, within 30 business days after the date of this notice. Your written request for the administrative review should be sent to the Division of Child Support Enforcement, P.O. Box 40408, Phoenix, Arizona 85067.

We received a total $571.94 in support for your case(s). We distributed the money as follows:

1. $0.00   paid to you for current support for the month(s) of Jul 14 – Sep 14

2. $571.94   paid to you for arrears owed to you. These arrears may have accrued after you stopped receiving public assistance.

3. $0.00   to DCSE to repay assigned arrears based on past public assistance you received. As of the date of this notice, DCSE claims an additional $0.00 for assigned arrears based on public assistance paid to you. **These amounts are combined totals for all of your child support cases and may not show all the public assistance paid to you.**

3a.   paid to   for assigned arrears based on past public assistance you
     paid to
     paid to
     paid to
     paid to
received.

4. $0.00   paid to DCSE for genetic testing fees.

5. $0.00   paid to DCSE for the monthly handling fee required by A.R.S. § 25-510.

About the Author

Almost as far back as Robin can recall, she aspired to be an esteemed author. Having survived staggering loss and abuse throughout her life, she taught herself how to heal, in spite of life's hostile conditions. Robin is a survivor and has become a motivational speaker and an outspoken advocate for victim's rights.

Notes

We are all perfectly, imperfect. Embrace the real you.

You will never speak to anyone more than you speak to yourself in your head. Be kind to yourself.

Life will always try to make things difficult for you, but every time you overcome obstacles, you come out stronger.

Amazing, unbelievably good things happen when you follow your gut, your truth, your passion, your heart.

Life throws you challenges. Rise up, face them head on and conquer!

Remember the truest love you will find is within yourself.

Survive and thrive